Mabil

Wol

Ama

Bill's
amp

Garrkany
Camp Site

Iliwara

Fishing
Place

Badpanawan
Jabiru
nest

AKADU

Forest

NATIONAL

PARK

East

Paperbark

Nadab – floodplain closeup
to Ubirr

Alligator

Monsoon

Forest

Ubirr

Galleries

I would like to give special thanks to all those who spent their time with my father and helped him tell his story,

to Stephen Davis and Allan Fox who contributed their texts from the previous editions of this book,

particular thanks to Stephen Davis for the many hours he spent with Bill transcribing the poems,

to Ian Morris, Greg Miles and Mark Lang who took the photographs,

and Jane Moore and Mark Lang who put it all together.

There is a good story within these pages.

Please read it well and learn from the wisdom within.

Jonathan Nadji, 2001
Son

Bunitj Clan
Kakadu National Park

I give you this story.
this proper, true story.
People can listen.
I'm telling this while you've got time,
time for you to make something,
you know,
history
book.

Gagudju Man
BILL NEIDJIE

*The environmental and spiritual philosophy of
a senior traditional owner
Kakadu National Park, Northern Territory, Australia*

GECKO
BOOKS

Bill Neidjie - Gagudju Man, this edition published in 2007 by:
Gecko Books (JP & PW Enterprises P/L)
PO Box 118
Marleston SA 5033
Phone +61 8 8351 1688 Fax +61 8 351 1699

Words   Bill Neidjie

Foreword   Ian Morris

Commentary   Stephen Davis, Allan Fox

Photography   **Mark Lang -** cover, panorama below and previous page;
panoramas on pages 2-3, 4-5, 70-71, 72-73, 74-75, 78-79, 82-83.
Greg Miles - pages 8, 58, 59, 60 (bottom), 62, 64 (turtles & goose), 68, 76-77, 80-81, backcover.
Ian Morris - introductory portrait of Bill Neidjie, pages 6, 7, 12, 60 (top), 64 (lower left), 66.
Ted Ryko - page 10 [courtesy Northern Territory Library Service].

Design, layout,
Editing   Jane Moore, Mark Lang

Artwork   Jane Moore

Proof reading Penelope Charlesworth

Printer   Produced by Phoenix Offset, Hong Kong

Royalty distribution for Bill Neidjie and or his family: Djabulukgu Association.

ISBN 978 09803522 38

National Library of Australia Cataloguing-in-publication data:
Neidjie, Bill, 1913-2002
Gagudju man.
1. Neidjie, Bill, 1913-2002. 2. Traditional ecological knowledge - Northern Territory - Kakadu National Park.
3. Aboriginal Australians - Northern Territory - Kakadu National Park. 4. Aboriginal Australians - Northern Territory - Social life and customs. 5. Kakadu National Park (N.T.) - Environmental conditions.
1. Title.

333.720994295

FOREWORD

BILL NEIDJIE IS UNIQUE among the Aboriginal people of Australia for a variety of profound reasons.

Firstly, he belongs to a long line of people who have managed one of the most beautiful and ecologically diverse regions remaining in Australia. His land now forms one of the jewels in the crown of the world renowned Kakadu National Park. Far sighted and wise, he follows his father, Ngadambala, who played a major role in assisting the first western enterprise on this landscape – buffalo shooting and the sale of hides.

Secondly, again following in his father's footsteps, Bill has had to continue the process of carefully teaching the ever-increasing number of non-Aboriginal people who wish to share the riches of his land. He belongs to two very different worlds. To this end, he is seen as something of a 'guru' to both sides.

Thirdly, Bill has found himself as the essential negotiator in the future of his father's land – the Bunitj Clan Estate. This responsibility is combined with the knowledge that he cannot prevent these changes. Outside pressures have constantly pushed him to take some part in altering the natural and cultural landscape which has nurtured his people over one of the longest periods of human history.

His land has seen significant natural changes over time – changes in the earth's surface, sea level, climate, vegetation and animal life, as well as fluctuations in human population. These events have gradually moulded the landscape into the richness we now call Kakadu. Bill's people have observed and recorded many of these changes in the story of their land – the story of their people.

And he knows that his generation has seen the greatest social and environmental changes over that entire period. This element of tragedy is always in the background of Bill's presence.

More so than his parents, his children and his grandchildren, he has witnessed the rapid demise of his people's way of life, their recorded history, their language, their personal cultural knowledge – in effect, their understanding of themselves.

Bill did something that was foreign to his forefathers. He went to the little mission school at Oenpelli, across the East Alligator River, opposite Bunitj land. He claims that he was a poor student and did not last very long before heading for the bush again. Over the years he has watched schools in Aboriginal communities replacing the traditional learning pathways of his people, even though he has tried hard to

teach his children and grandchildren the ways of old. In his long lifetime he has watched this knowledge fade in importance to the younger generations as the ways of the world crowd in. At the same time, most of his friends and traditional associates have passed on, leaving him culturally isolated. In his old age he has had to face a vastly altered future, the sad legacy of all elderly Aboriginal people in today's world.

Nevertheless, Bill is an optimist. He can brush away sadness with his infectious laugh. Despite the limitations of poor health, Bill likes nothing better than telling stories or sharing his philosophies on the relationship between humans and the land. Many visitors to Kakadu National Park have had their experiences greatly enriched by meeting Big Bill Neidjie – Gagudju Man.

I count it as a privilege to have known and lived alongside Bill in his latter years. He is a great mentor, work associate, and more particularly, an unselfish friend who enjoys sharing his inheritance unconditionally. This generosity makes me wonder what Australia may have been like if we had listened to the wisdom of people like Bill from the point of western colonisation.

In this book, Bill relives the past in order to give some meaningful structure to the future. It is an attempt to help non-Aboriginal people understand the bond between Aboriginal people and their traditionally inherited land. It is for Bill's descendants as well as ours. He knows that every human being has the responsibility of caring for the land. He also knows that in the days to come, many other people will be making decisions for the land he now speaks for.

This is his way of speaking into the future. All of us who read these thoughts will also carry that responsibility.

Kakadu National Park is the scenic, scientific and culturally diverse place it is today because of people like Bill. I hope, like myself, you enjoy some of the unique cultural insight that this book contains.

IAN MORRIS
'Riyala',
Northern Territory
November 2001

BILL NEIDJIE

ARCHAEOLOGICAL WORK in the East Alligator River area evidences a continuous occupation of the region by Aboriginal people for the last 25,000 years. Such work also confirms that pigments for painting were prepared at least 18,000 years ago.

During the glacial period of 20,000 years ago, when the coast was a further 250 kilometres north and the flood plains perhaps 100 metres above the sea level, the Aboriginal people were fresh-water river people occupying the Alligator Rivers areas. With the melting of the glaciers, the sea level rose and the Alligator Rivers environment changed. As the sea approached its present day level, the area became estuarine and Aboriginal people ranged across a landscape – including water lilies and geese – similar to that which we see today.

Aboriginal occupation of the Alligator Rivers area has embraced a time span beyond which most people can conceive. When Moses was leading the exodus from Egypt, Aboriginal occupation of the Alligator Rivers had been continuous for at least 218 centuries. When Christ was embarking on his ministry in Galilee, Aboriginal people had occupied the Alligator Rivers for almost 230 centuries

The arrival of Captain James Cook in Australia had been preceded, then, by over 250 centuries of continuous occupation in the Alligator Rivers. This occupation included what has been identified in recorded history as the estate of the Gagudju (Kakadu) people, and in particular the Bunitj Clan estate of Big Bill Neidjie.

The earliest accounts of European contact with the Gagudju come from the explorer Ludwig Leichhardt. In November and December of 1844, Leichhardt and his party travelled through the area noting that the country was well populated.

> *The natives were very numerous and employing themselves either in fishing or burning the grass on the plains, or digging for roots. I saw here a noble fig-tree, under the shade of which seemed to have been the camping place of the natives for the last century.*
> (Leichhardt 1847: 493)

The total Aboriginal population of the area at the time of Leichhardt's contact was probably in excess of 2,000 people.

Following European contact, a serious decline in the population took place. In 1922 Paddy Cahill, a well-known buffalo hunter in the region, stated that he would not be able to muster more than a hundred Aborigines in the area.

Census figures for the 1960s confirmed fears that there were few local people alive. A census return for 1965 lists only two Gagudju people as well as Charlie Whittaker (an elderly Aboriginal friend of Bill Neidjie listed as belonging to the 'Gunwinggo' tribe). A 1966 census listed only Bill's close friend Felix Holmes (Iyanuk) of the Limilngan language group and two elderly Gagudju people in the area.
Bill Neidjie is one of the few of the remaining Gagudju.

Big Bill Neidjie was born at Alawanydajawany on the East Alligator River in the mid 1920s or earlier. Bill, like his father Nadampala before him, is of the Bunitj clan (*gunmugurrkurr*), Gagudju language group.

Bill was raised in the East Alligator area. He lived at Ubirr for maybe one year when his mother, Lucy Wirlmaka, was about 21 years old. Here he learnt to hunt and to manage the resources of his environment. His father, his grandfather and his uncles instructed Bill in Gagudju law.

While Bill was still a child his mother stencilled his hand in ochre on a rock shelter at the site known as Walkarr, on the Bunitj clan estate, where it remains today.

Bill's mother, from the Ulbuk clan of the Amurrak language group, took Bill to live at Cape Don 180 kilometres north of East Alligator when Bill was 12 or 13 years of age. He lived there with his mother's family for 5 or 6 years. 'Old Billy Manilugu, we lived with him. He was a buffalo hunter. He knew all the (Aboriginal) law.'

Billy Manilungu was a prominent ceremonial leader throughout the entire region. 'He was a big song man.' Billy Manilugu taught Bill much of the traditional

These photos of the Northern Territory buffalo industry were taken by Ryko when Bill was a small boy. [Northern Territory & Information Service]

Aboriginal law. After the Second World War he particularly taught Bill's friend, Iyanuk (Felix Holmes) of the Limilngan Clan, many of the songs necessary for the continuance of the Morak ceremonial cycle of which Bill and Iyanuk are custodians.

Bill returned to East Alligator intermittently until he was about 20 years of age. At that time Bill's mother took up residence at Cape Don on a permanent basis where she stayed until her mother passed away.

As a young man in company with his friend Toby Gangali of the Mirrarr clan, Bill started work with the buffalo hunters at Cannon Hill but did not stay long. 'Me and Toby, we used to run away from them buffalo hunters. We were too young.'

From about 22 years of age, Bill worked for several years at a timber mill in Mountnorris Bay ('Iwal, that's near Minimini Creek') for Chan Long. Bill then was engaged to cart timber to Darwin in the lugger *Maskee*. The work continued from Mountnorris Bay until the mill at Croker Island took over. Bill worked with the Croker mill for a further three years. 'There was no mission there then. Soon as war came, mission started for coloured people.'

Bill then started work with Leo Hickey on his lugger along the north coast run. On one occasion, Leo Hickey, with Bill in his employ, was engaged to transport 20 to 30 people to the new settlement of Maningrida. But, as Bill relates, the task was not entirely successful. 'They did not stay there because after two weeks there were no smokes (cigarettes) left.'

During the Second World War, Bill returned to the East Alligator area where he lived at Paw Paw Beach (Murgenella Creek). There, an Ubarr ceremony was performed. Participation in an Ubarr ceremony is one of the most important events in a Gagudju man's life. Ruben Cooper, the son by an Aboriginal woman, of one of the first European buffalo hunters, was a senior man overseeing that particular performance of the Ubarr ceremony.

'Ruben Cooper told me to get in that Ubarr. Otherwise it would be too late for me and I would miss it. He said, "In two weeks when you finished that ceremony you come and see me." Two dozen of us young fellers went in (to be initiated into the ceremony).' Bill and fellow initiates were under the control of senior ceremonial leaders. Severe restrictions are placed on initiates who are isolated during the performance of the Ubarr ceremony, including eating and drinking prohibitions. 'Those old men never even let us move. They tell us, "See that big well over there? We'll put you in it and you'll be dead if you disobey." But three men were waiting for us ... with spears. "Where you going?" they say. We were so scared we was shaking all over.'

Some time later, Ruben Cooper became ill. 'There was no medicine so he died. But, half way before he died, he said to me, "I don't know if I'll see you again. You look after the land." Then he died.'

In recent years Bill has again become a permanent resident on his own land. In 1979 Bill was a claimant in the Alligator Rivers Stage II Land Claim heard before Justice Toohey, the Aboriginal Land Commissioner. The Bunitj people of the Gagudju language group were awarded title to their land as a result of this claim.

The identity of an Aboriginal person, however, is much more than legal title to land. He must fulfil the responsibilities with which his people were charged by ancestral beings in the creative epoch.

For Gagudju Man, Big Bill Neidjie, land is life.

1981

Post Script

Ruben, Charlie, Felix, and Toby are gone. Their spirits have gone back to their country. Big Bill is the last of the old Gagudju. But his dream has come true ...... the title to Bunitj land is secure and a new generation of Gagudju is growing up with Gagudju law.

I belong to this earth.
Soon my bones become earth ... all the same.
My spirit has gone back to my country ... my mother.
Now my children got to hang onto this story ...
I hang onto this story all my life.
My children can't lose it.

This law,
This country,
This people,
All the same ...
Gagudju.

STEPHEN DAVIS, 2001

The Words of Bill Neidjie

'I Give You This Story'

I give you this story,
this proper, true story.
People can listen.
I'm telling this while you've got time,
time for you to make something,
you know,
history
book.

I was thinking.
No history written for us
when white European start here,
only few words written.
Should be more than that.

Should be written way Aborigine was live.
That floodplain.
My father, my mother, my grandfather
all used to hunt there, use ironwood spear.
No clothes then.

When I was growing up
good mob of people all around then.
Now people bit wicked.
My time never do little bit wrong,
otherwise get spear straight away.
Now, little bit cheeky mob.
Old time they would all be dead now.
Old people were hard.
I frightened when young.
Only few people now,
But it easy for this mob.

Anyway, got to be made that book.
There's still time.
No man can growl at me for telling this story,
because it will be too late.
I'll be dead.

He can't move his country

This earth
I never damage.
I look after.
Fire is nothing,
just clean up.
When you burn,
new grass coming up.
That mean good animal soon.
Might be goose, long-neck turtle, goanna, possum.
Burn him off,
new grass coming up,
new life all over.

I don't know about white European way.
We, Aborigine, burn.
Make things grow.
Tree grow,
every night he grow.
Daylight
he stop.
Just about dark,
he start again.
Just about morning, I look.
I say, 'Oh, nice tree this.'

When you sleep,
tree growing like other trees,
they got lots of blood.

Rotten tree,
you got to burn him.
Use him to cook.
He's finished up,
cook or roast in coals,
White man cook in oven,
From university that.
Aborigine didn't know that before.
Now all this coming up with Toyota.

First people come to us,
they started and run our life... quick.
They bring drink.
First they should ask about fish, cave, dreaming,
but
they rush in.
They make school. Teach.

Now Aborigine losing it,
losing everything.
Nearly all dead my people,
my old people gone.

Those first people was too quick,
wasn't Aborigine fault.
Still Aborigine all around 1929,
1952, 1953 few left but...
1970 to 1979... gone.
Only me, Robin Gaden and Felix Holmes.

Each man he stay,
stay on his own country.
He can't move his country
so he stay there,
stay with his language.
Language is different,
like skin.
Skin can be different,
but blood same.

Blood and bone,
all same.
Man can't split himself.

White European can't say,
'Oh, that Aborigine no good.'
Might be that Aborigine alright.
Man can't growl at Aborigine,
Aborigine can't growl at white European.
Because both ways.
Might be both good men,
might be both no good.
You never know.

So you should get understand yourself.
No matter Aborigine or white European.

I was keeping this story myself.
It was secret in my mind
but I see what other people doing,
and I was feeling sad.

Law

Law never change,
always stay same.
Maybe it hard,
but proper one for all people.

Not like white European law,
always changing.
If you don't like it,
you can change.

Aboriginal law never change.
Old people tell us,
'You got to keep it.'
It always stays.

Creek, plain, hill.
That plain can change.
Wet season, him mud.
You get lily,
you get fish.
But, he dry up...
that's alright.
Then people can get long-neck turtle.
Same for animal.
People look for food,
animal look for food.
Lizard look,
bird look,
anyone look.
We all same.

Each billabong can be dry...
no fish, turtle, nothing.
He want new water,
then fish and turtle,
make him new one.
New rain coming up,
That rain make everything again.
Plenty fish, turtle, lily.

Rain for us, for anybody.
Rain give us everything new.
Yam, fish, everything.

Barramundi good in the wet season,
still good after the wet because of rain.
Big barramundi from salt water.
He follow fresh water down river,
rain helping him.
He can make eggs.

We must get rain.
Law says we get rain.
He come along wet season
and go dry season.
Rain come down
and give us new fresh water.
Plants coming up new.
Yam, creeper, all plants new.
Then we get fruit, honey and things to live.

Tree, he change with rain.
He get new leaf,
he got to come because rain.
Yam he getting big too.

Old people say
'You dig yam?
Well you digging your granny or mother
through the belly.
You must cover it up,
cover again.
When you get yam you cover over,
then no hole through there.
Yam can grow again.'

'You hang onto this story,' they say.
So I hang on.
I tell kids.
When they get yam, leave hole.
I say
'Who leave that hole?
Cover him up!'
They say
'We forget.'
I tell them
'You leaving hole.
You killing yam.
You killing yourself.
You hang onto your country.
That one I fight for.
I got him.
Now he's yours.
I'll be dead,
I'll be coming to earth.'

All these places for us,
all belong Gagudju.
We use them all the time.
Old people used to move around,
camp different place.
Wet season, dry season,
always camp different place.
Wet season
we camp high place,
get plenty goose egg.
No trouble for fresh water.

Dry season,
move along floodplain
billabong got plenty food.
Even food there when everything dry out.

All Gagudju used to visit,
used to come here to billabong,
dry season camp.
Plenty file snake, long-neck turtle.
Early dry season,
good lily.
Just about middle dry season
file snake, long-neck turtle,
lily flowering.

Everybody camp,
like holiday.
Plenty food this place.
Good time for ceremony,
stay maybe one or two weeks.

Pelican, Jabiru, White Cockatoo,
all got to come back,
make him like before.

Fish,
he listen.
He say,
'Oh, somebody there.'
Him frightened, too many Toyota.
Make me worry too.

I look after my country,
now lily coming back.
Lily, nuts, birds, fish.
Whole lot coming back.

We got to look after,
can't waste anything.
We always used what we got,
old people and me.

If man leave one or two barramundi behind
he go bad.
Trouble,
big fight.
He can't waste anything.
My culture's hard,
but got to be to keep him.
If you waste him anything now,
Next year you can't get as much
because you already waste.

When I was young I never wasted,
otherwise straight away I get trouble.
Even bone not wasted,
Make soup or burn that bone.
Watch out...
That might be dreaming one too.

That story change him now.
It should still be,
but young people won't listen.
Just chuck him away.
Waste him,
destroy everything.

When we young...
my time, Felix's time,
we never eat big fish.
That fish for old people.

Same for goose.
Young people only eat shoulder of goose,
older people must have goose first.
Same for Oenpelli, Mary River, all over.
If young people eat goose or fish,
then he'll be dead.
No young people touch him big fish or goose.
If touch him,
law says got to die.

You know frill-neck lizard?
He look funny.
Used to be good smooth animal.
He was man.
He done something wrong.
Look ugly now... skinny leg, arm,
big one ear, frill-neck.
What he done?
Break law.

He went to sacred ceremony....
called Ubarr.
He didn't listen,
clapping hands.
Old people tell him
'You break law,
you'll be skinny,
you won't grow more.
People will see you like that.'

And he went like that...
big ear.
'You'll be like that for ever and ever.'

Lizard say,
'You make me back like I was before.'
People say 'No,
you break law.
You got to stay like that,
it's law.'

We can't break law.
No, we can't break law.
That frill-neck lizard done it first,
now look how thin he is.
That his own fault.
He spoilt ceremony.

We can't change it.
That's law.

Land

People.
they can't listen for us.
They just listen for money.
Money.

We want goose, we want fish.
Other men want money.
Him can make million dollars,
but only last one year.
Next year him want another million.
Forever and ever him make million dollars.
Him die.

Million no good for us.
We need this earth to live because
we'll be dead,
we'll become earth.

This ground and this earth,
like brother and mother.

Trees and eagle.
You know eagle?
He can listen.
Eagle our brother,
like dingo our brother.

We like this earth to stay,
because he was staying for ever and ever.

We don't want to lose him.
We say 'Sacred, leave him.'

Goanna is dead
because they cutting its body off us,
cutting our mother's belly,
grandpa's bones.
They squash him up.
No good,
And carve up our earth.
No good.

We come from earth, bones.
We go to earth, ashes.

My children got to hang onto this story.
This important story.
I hang onto this story all my life.
My father tell me this story.
My children can't lose it.

White European want to know
asking 'What this story?'
This not easy story.
No-one else can tell it
because this story for Aboriginal culture.

I speak English for you,
so you can listen,
so you can know,
you will understand.
If I put my language in same place,
you won't understand.

Our story is in the land.
It is written in those sacred places.
My children will look after those places,
that's the law.

No-one can walk close to those sacred places.
No difference for Aborigine or white European,
that's the law.
We can't break law.

Old people tell me,
'You got to keep law.'
'What for?' I said.
'No matter we die but that law,
you got to keep it.
No camping in secret place,
no fire there,
no play for kids.
You can't break law.
Law must stay.'

When that law started?
I don't know how many thousands of years.
European say 40,000 years,
but I reckon myself probably was more
because...
it is sacred.

Dreaming place,
you can't change it,
no matter who you are.
No matter you rich man,
no matter you king.
You can't change it.

We say that's secret because dreaming there.
We frightened you might get hurt if you go there,
not only my country but any secret place.
No matter if it Croker Island, Elcho Island,
Brisbane or Sydney.

Wherever, you'll get him same
because that secret place not small.
Secret place is biggest one.
Everywhere.
Powerful.

We walk on earth,
we look after,
like rainbow sitting on top.
But something underneath,
under the ground.
We don't know.
You don't know.

What you want to do?
If you touch,
you might get cyclone, heavy rain or flood.
Not just here,
you might kill someone in another place.
Might be kill him in another country.
You cannot touch him.

These very important places,
but we frightened that European might touch him.
If we tell white European story,
he slow to listen.
If we get little bit wild,
he might listen. But slow.

Him got to always ask question.
He want that place.
That's why we frightened.
I worry about that place.
Secret place.
That got painting there, inside cave.
It got to be looked after because
my father, grandad all look after.
Now me,
I got to do same.
If that painting get rubbed off
there might be big trouble.
That important story.
It for all round this area.
That biggest story,
biggest place.

My grandpa teach me.
That painting is true.
Fish, python, goose,
all painting there.
Grandpa say
'You see painting,
Fish, you got to eat.
Python, you got to eat.
Mullet, you got to eat.
Lily, turtle, all same.
They for you.'

That drawing there, painting,
that's the size fish should be now.
Used to be that size.
I saw them myself.
Used to be that size at Oenpelli
Need two men to carry one catfish.
That was when I was nearly man,
still young.

Now?
Little boy can carry catfish.
Should be fifty pounds,
but only fifteen pounds.

You can't see big fish anymore,
not at Oenpelli.
People say, 'Plenty fish there.
You see barramundi.'

I say
'Yes, pocket fish.'
They say
'What you mean?'
I tell them,
'Pocket fish that barramundi,
little one.
You can put him in your pocket.'

They tell me
'Big catfish,
we got him plenty.'
I say
'Should be ten times size of that.'

We have to keep pressure on young people to learn.
They must learn these things.
I have to stay on to teach my children.
But, young people spread out.
It like that every time we have meetings,
meeting for ceremony.
We make arrangement...
you know... appointment,
about business, secret.
Young people all in town.

You look now...
Nobody with me.
This old man here (Iyanuk, Felix Holmes)
he with me,
but we don't have a dozen behind us.
So, we must stay on.
Look after and teach.

All my uncle gone,
but this story I got him.
They told me.
They taught me
and I can feel it.

I feel it with my body,
with my blood.
Feeling all these trees,
all this country.
When this wind blow you can feel it.
Same for country,
You feel it.
You can look.
But feeling...
that make you.

Feeling make you.
Out there in open space,
he coming through your body.
Look while he blow and feel with your body,
because tree just about your brother or father
and tree is watching you.

Earth.
Like your father or brother or mother,
because you born from earth.
You got to come back to earth.
When you dead,
you'll come back to earth.
Maybe little while yet...
then you'll come to earth.
That's your bone, your blood.
It's in this earth,
same as for tree.

Tree.
He watching you.
You look at tree,
he listen to you.
He got no finger,
he can't speak.

But that leaf,
he pumping, growing,
growing in the night.

While you sleeping
you dream something.
Tree and grass same thing.
They grow with your body,
with your feeling.

If you feel sore,
headache, sore body,
that mean somebody killing tree or grass.

You feel
because your body in that tree or earth.
Nobody can tell you,
you got to feel it yourself.

Tree might be sick,
you feel it.
You might feel it for two or three years.
You get weak,
little bit, little bit.
Because tree going bit by bit.
Dying.

Tree not die when you cut it.
He not die tomorrow, he still green.
Might be five or six weeks,
might be two months.
You feel it then.

Your body.
You feel it.

Environment

Those trees,
they grow and grow.
Every night they grow.
That grass,
no matter it burn.
When it drink,
it grow again.
When you cut tree,
it pump life away,
all the same as blood in my arm.

Earth,
same thing.
You brought up with earth, tree, water.

Water is your blood.
Water,
you can't go without water.
No matter no food two days,
three day, four day,
if you got water.
If no water,
little bit weak,
getting hard.
Water important.

That's why we get story.
Old people tell us about that first lightning.
That's before wet season.
We can't look at it.
Later we get lightning and rain from other way.
But, must not look at first lightning,
bend head down
like first woman who looked.
She was ashamed and bent her head.
We must do the same.

Sky,
cloud.
Made for us.
Star,
he'll stay for ever and ever.

When you lying down in the night,
look at star.

I was lying down,
I look star.
It make me remember when I was young.

When young I think that star really river,
river and creek.
You call it Southern Cross,
that other star.
We say it spear and crocodile.

So, I just look.
I remember other star,
eagle,
eagle on other side.

I look at star.
I know just about time for wet season,
may be time for dry season.
I know from star.

Well now that star over here,
so look out for wet season.
That star right down in December.
When that wet season come,
that star come back.
I say, 'Well, dry season coming.'
Then rain finish him up.

October
up high.
November
getting low.
December
right down.

My grandpa taught me that.
He said,
'Don't forget this.
Tell this story with kids
so he can listen
slow.

And then story will come for him,
exactly like this.
This story right, exactly right,
because it dreaming.'

Death

We all lying down on grass in dry season.
Look up at stars.
I tell kids,
'See them stars.
They been there million years.
They always be there.'

I see pink star.
I tell them 'That King Brown Snake.'
I see his eye,
that pink one.
That star he work.
He go pink, white, pink, white.
That King Brown he look at night.

Eagle, star,
we got him story.
What you call him?
Mars that one,
really eagle.
One arm short,
left wing long one.
His wing been burnt.

Three or four kind of eagle here.
Proper one really that black one.
He can kill him black wallaby.
Proper eagle that one.
Other one with white chest,
he can go billabong or salt water.
But, black one proper eagle.

I look at moon.
It tell me story, like stars.
Moon,
moon is man.
He said,
'These people will die,
but they'll come back
like I do.
They'll come back to be earth again.'

Native Cat said 'No,
they will be dead and never come back.'
Everyone jump on him and kill him.
They burn him so he got plenty spots.
Spots from hot coals.

So moon say again
'Man will come back,
like I come back each time.
He'll come back to earth.'

I know I come back to my country.
When I die I become earth.
I love this country and this earth.

This story for all people.
Everybody should be listening.
Same story for everyone,
just different language.

My meaning might be little bit hard,
so I speak English.
You just listen careful...
slow.

We got to hang on
not to lose our story.
Don't think about money too much.
You can get million dollar,
but not worth it.
Million dollar,
he just go 'poof'.
Couple of weeks,
you got nothing.

This ground never move.
I'll be buried here.
I'll be with my brother, my mother.
If I lose this,
where I'll be buried?
I'm hanging onto this ground.
I'll become earth again.
I belong to this earth.
And earth should stay with us.

Tree the same as me.
When he get old he'll die.
He'll be dead and burn.
He'll leave his ashes behind.
Tree become earth.

When I die,
I become skeleton.
I'll be in cave.
That way my spirit stay there.

I seen new coffin three or four times.
No good.
I don't want coffin,
just cave.

Should be keep our law.

Coffin no good for Aborigine,
got to put bones back where they belong.
Man die.
Soon as him ready,
pick him up,
take him.
Take him to cave.
His shadow,
his spirit,
will stay with him.

If you go in cave
you must call out.
If you've got young man with you,
he might be stranger for that cave,
for that spirit.

You got to call out first.
You must signal,
must sing out
because old people used to tell us,
'Your father,
your grandad,
your aunty,
they'll be waiting for you.
Call out,
they'll listen.
They'll know you,
and they say,
That stranger
we can't hurt him.'

Old people tell me,
'When you dead you'll be buried.
Uncle bury you in sacred place.'

They told me,
'Don't be rough in your life.
If you too rough,
little bit mistake.'
I said 'What mistake?
No-one can kill me with spear.'
They say
'Yes, we know,
nobody kill you on outside.'

'No mark in your body.
But inside,
when you feeling sick,
sick in your body.
Headache is nothing.
But in your body,
get very bad sick.'
I ask, 'Why?'
They say,
'See that big tree?'
I said
'Yes, I chop him down that tree.
I play,
I cut him.'

'You cut yourself,' they say.
'When you maybe forty years,
might be fifty years old,
you feel pain in your back,
because you cut tree.
I'm old man,' he said,
I'm telling you.'

Land got to stay,
always stay same.
No matter little track,
grass still grow,
bush can grow.

But soon as bitumen there,
all finished.

Grass don't grow,
Maybe little bit side,
but middle... nothing.
You look where timber
gone,
pulled out.
Bulldozer rip it out.

Well, you feel it in your body.
You say,
'That tree same as me.'
This piece of ground he grow you.

Conclusion

Rock stays,
earth stays.

I die and put my bones in cave or earth.
Soon my bones become earth,
all the same.

My spirit has gone back to my country,
my mother.

This story is important.
It won't change,
it is law.
It is like this earth,
it won't move.

Ground and rock,
he can't move.
Cave,
he never move.
No-one can shift that cave,
because it dream.
It story.
It law.

This law,
this country,
this people,
No matter what people,
red, yellow, black or white,
the blood is the same.
Lingo little bit different,
but no matter.
Country,
you in other place.
But same feeling.
Blood, bone,
all the same.

This story,
this is true story.

My people
all dead.
We only got few left.
That's all, not many.
We getting too old.

Young people.
I don't know if they can hang onto this story.

But, now you know this story,
and you'll be coming to earth.
You'll be part of earth when you die.
You responsible now.
You got to go with us.
To earth.
Might be you can hang on.
Hang onto this story.
To this earth.

You got children,
grandson.
Might be your grandson will get this story,
keep going,
hang on like I done.

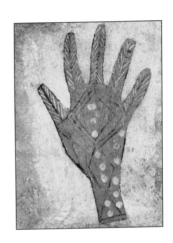

THE BEGINNING

THE OCCUPATION OF AUSTRALIA by humans probably began as long ago as 65,000 years when, during a period of low sea level, a small group of coastal people made a remarkable ocean voyage across the final gap separating this land from the Indonesian lowlands. Noone will ever know what drove these people on. It may have been population pressure which was the direct cause now that the vast inter-island Sunda plains had been exposed by the retreating sea of an ice age. Or was it the seasonal drift of smoke from fires burning in the greatly increased area of woodlands from over the south-eastern horizon, which lured them on? Did the steady north-west monsoon which, along with bamboo, and other flotsam – including people on flimsy rafts – simply drive them here, like it drove the later Maccassans, Vietnamese and the boat people from Middle East.

Whatever the reason, these were people of the coasts, people who lived by the sea and with the sea. Once they had conquered the problem of flotation, their arrival was inevitable. They arrived, not as an invading force and not as purposeful colonists, but as 'lost' people saved when they beached on the long low mangrove-covered shores of north-western Australia. Whatever their mode of arrival, they came long, long ago, perhaps two thousand generations before the pyramids were built.

Eight generations ago, Cook's belated 'discoveries' set in motion the forces which have all but destroyed this Aboriginal culture, a culture rooted in 65,000 years experience of the Australian environment.

A vision of the richness and depth of that experience comes through in Big Bill Neidjie's wisdom. But we get ahead of our story.

It is most likely that the Ancestor Aboriginals arrived at a time when a glacial period was in full swing. The sea level had dropped some 100 metres. The last time the levels were as low as that was between 15,000 and 20,000 years ago. However, at that time people were grinding their tools near the caverns by the East Alligator (a world first in technology), and Aborigines had been camping by Lake Mungo for at least 30,00 and more years. The low sea level previous to the last was between 50,000 and 55,000 years ago. That then is a likely arrival period.

Even with these low sea levels the trip to Australia required a substantial voyage of up to ninety kilometres, perhaps making the Ancestors the first mariners. They landed on a combined North Australian New Guinean coast which was then seawards 300-500 kilometres north-west of the present coast.

The beach and what lay ahead was a vast unknown plain in the minds of these very early navigators. The oceanic gap separated the Australian realm from the Asian. Tigers and leopards gave way to thylacines and marsupial lions; buffalo, rhinoceros and pigs to diprotodons, kangaroos, and wallabies; monkeys to koalas, possums and phalangers. Now two worlds had drifted close enough for humans to enter and be nonplussed by the old Australian creatures. Some northern animals, the rodents and bats for instance, had made it earlier while some other animals – the crocodiles and turtles for example – were common to both worlds.

But like Neil Armstrong or Columbus, those first settlers must have found Australia and New Guinea a new and mysterious place.

The first people were navigators with a tradition of food, shelter and understandings which were coastal. As the Ancestors moved about the land, they saw, remembered and explained the features. So far as humans were concerned, their discoveries created a 'new' landscape, just as Columbus had 'created' the Americas for Spaniards.

As a child builds up a perception of place through accumulated experience, so too did these early generations accumulate perceptions of landscape – of their habitat. Place was associated with natural phenomena, in particular, powerful elements such as lightning, floods, fire and volcanoes. Over time, this growing net of perceptions were given authority and coherence and effectively passed on from generation to generation by being linked with, creation heroes. The environment and humans were gradually being seen as parts of the same processes of the living world.

Bird, he gone now. He was talking. He gone.
He say goodnight, he go sleep might be.

All kind of animal come to you because that mean you
got story, and they know your story.
That not really bird, but spirit, spirit of these people.
They were camping here, and they watching us,
to look after us, might be.

Good for them, and good for you.

Make you good.

Good feeling.

Over the generations, traditions of the people became increasingly complex. These traditions were woven into the structure of society, into the relationships between people, and between people and their habitat. Accumulated experience became so great that even the oldest individual could not retain it all. Without a written language this wisdom of the people remained in many living minds. These minds were living in a landscape every part of which was a permanent reminder of perception and explanation. This information was passed on from generation to generation. So it is that the modern Aboriginal person inherits a culture where landscape is critical to maintaining physical, mental and spiritual life. Key parts of the landscape are referred to as 'sacred sites' – but does the word 'sacred' have the depth of meaning that can convey the values attached to these places?

So, through 50,000 or more years, the environment which sustained life and culture, became bound intimately with every aspect of human life. Aboriginal and environment were one and the same. Ownership of land in the European sense did not exist: Aboriginal people were part of the living systems. Through their mythology they understood that their Ancestors created the landscape and the life on it. This life included themselves, with each person playing a role in the maintenance of the whole dynamic world: this was key to the maintenance of their community and to their continued survival.

The most important role that an individual human could play in this system was that of custodian of the common environment. First chairman of the Northern LandCouncil, Silas Roberts, put it this way:

> *Aboriginals have a special connection with everything that is natural. Aboriginals see themselves as part of nature. We see all things natural as part of us. All the things on Earth we see as part-human. This is told through the idea of dreaming. By dreaming we mean the belief that long ago these creatures started human society.*

> *These creatures, these great creatures, are just as much alive today as they were in the beginning. They are everlasting and will never die. They are always part of the land and nature as we are. Our connection to all things natural is spiritual.*

Stephen Davis, while teaching at Milingimbi, Arnhem Land, made many offshore fishing trips with local Aboriginal people. He soon became aware that his hosts avoided some areas of water and consistently turned back when the boat drifted across seemingly imaginary lines. When asked for an explanation, the people shrugged and said that the place was someone else's land. Triangulating features

All Gagudju used to visit,
used to come here to billabong,
dry season camp.

Plenty file snake, long-neck turtle.
Early dry season,
good lily.

Just about middle dry season
file snake, long-neck turtle,
lily flowering.

Everybody camp,
like holiday.

Plenty food this place.
Good time for ceremony,
stay maybe one or two weeks.

Pelican, Jabiru, White Cockatoo,
all got to come back,
make him like before.

Top above: Magpie Goose.
Left: bush berries (rich in Vitamin C).
Above: the long necked turtle.

along the coast from the boat, Davis found that these places of turnaround were indeed consistent. Davis made many miles of soundings along the north coast and around Bathurst and Melville Islands. In each instance he found that the 'imaginary' lines actually follow undersea ridges and valley bottoms. His findings showed that, accurately bound into traditional behaviour, is knowledge of ice-age geography, of a landscape that disappeared five thousand years before the birth of Christ. To this day, some places under 30 metres of water are maintained as cased sites. To coastal people, land and water are one and the same. Tradition has it that, although the sea has had them in retreat, one day they will return to their submerged land.

With rising sea levels following melting of the ice, the meandering lower reaches of the Alligator Rivers became tidal estuaries. Mud built up along banks, cutting off side backswamps and mudflats. Sands were swept by wave, current and tide into bars and spits – building beach ridges between points, cutting off the sea and forming lagoon systems. Each bar, ridge and lagoon formed new zones for life. The mangroves moved in, becoming the habitat for more than twenty species, along with the animal components of these rich nurseries of marine life.

Geography and seasonality ruled the Aboriginal lives through their effect on access and food supply. This occured, not so much by controlling the supply of food, but by maintaining the variety as seasonal changes ushered in new foods. The Aboriginal seasonal calendar, based on six seasons, emphasises this point and today is increasingly acknowledged and worked with by land managers in the Top End of the Northern Territory. To indicate the complex ecological understandings which have developed, I quote from the Arnhem Land Environ Series published by the Milingimbi Literature Production Centre, Book 4, **Rrarranhdharr.**

> We know that Dharratharramirri (season) is coming to an end when balgurr (Brachychiton paradoxis) starts to lose its leaves. At the same time the pandanus (Gunga: Pandanusyirrkalensis) starts to fruit and Dhimurru (East- South -East) wind blows. The really cold mornings and mists are nearly gone. Sharks are giving birth to their young. They are called burrugu and so we call this season Burrugumirri. This is a very short season which only lasts for a few weeks. Stingrays are also called burrugu at this time. If munydjutj (Buchanania obovata) is flowering, then we are really sure that they are fat.

How fascinating it is to see the flowering of a plant as an indicator of stingrays being fat! How much experience and memory was needed to distil that relationship. This deeply integrated view of the human environment rests on the fact that the Aboriginal landscape has become fully personalised.

But how is such a store of tradition passed on, particularly without a written language? It happens primarily because life and learning are synonymous. Even a cursory look at the Bunitj year will illustrate the point. Tradition is continuously demonstrated and practised as a staged learning process, culminating at its richest point at the moment of death. Transmission is by way of myth, stories, field experiences, play, song cycles, dances, the pattern and design of artefacts along with the ritual of ceremonies.

The form of the area and its biota is seen to reflect the activities of the Ancestors. In the beginning, the Bunitj land, Bill Neidjie's land, was a blank plain. An Ancestral Being, Indjuwanydjuwa, travelled this landscape. His daily activities of hunting, gathering food and performing rituals, gave form to the landscape. He lived in a rock shelter on the wall on which was a painting depicting him. Following his acts of creation he turned himself into a great stone standing in a billabong surrounded by a sea of pink lotus lilies.

Today on Bunitj land, a chain of sites of varying importance defines the route of Indjuwanydjuwa's travels. The maintenance of these sites, along with their stories, rituals and songs, is the responsibility of the senior man of the clan.

A number of Ancestral Beings may have been involved in the creation of the landscape and its biota, including the humans. Some of these Beings were female, one of whom was involved in the birth of the Bunitj language group.

Some of the movements of other Ancestors took them into and across lands occupied by adjoining clans and therefore the stories and ceremonies related to these movements are shared and jointly enacted.

The coastal lowlands of the East Alligator River have been exposed by the retreating sandstone Arnhem Land Plateau. At lower sea levels the river cuts broad valleys in the ancient basement rocks. In places, isolated outliers of sandstone rise like islands from the lowland ridges. Subsequently the broad valleys fill with mud and became swampy plains. During wet seasons these plains become a vast wetland and as much as half of the Bunitj land goes under water.

Four distinct food producing zones are used at varying times according to the seasons: black soil floodplain, the stone country of the outliers and plateau, monsoon forest and eucalypt woodland forests. Before the coming of non-Aboriginals probably 40 to 60 people lived on this area, a number augmented from time to time by visits from adjoining clans. Some camps, as at Ubirr, were regularly used by eight clans, but always after permission had been sought from the traditional owner.

Movement was initiated by changes in food supply and the seasons, attendance at ceremonies and the need to be comfortable in this harsh environment. A man walking alone would cover 15 to 30 kilometres a day while a family with children would travel 8 to 10 kilometres between camps. Some traditional walks which linked people into a sequence of ceremonial activities and renewal of relationships with country, were of considerable magnitude– the Badmardi Clan of Kakadu had a recorded two month marathon of some 600 kilometres.

One could write much more about the depth of knowledge these people have about the natural community to which they and we belong. They are continually learning the processes of living – the landscape itself is not only teacher but textbook as well. In every physical and metaphysical way the Aboriginal people are inextricably bound to their land. These ecosystems were also, to varying degrees, artefacts of the relationship between land and humans, the use of fire as a tool being an obvious example of this process.

I can find no adequate word in English to describe the personalisation of the landscape by Aboriginals. It is little wonder then, that when Europeans arrived, had no capacity to understand these people. These new arrivals did not look for harmonious relationships and complex community structures which created relationships more akin to membership. Instead they looked for evidence of ownership, of manipulation, of control. Many still do.

The words of Big Bill Neidjie are an attempt by an old Aboriginal custodian to pass on to all people some of the wisdom accumulated from the experience of 2000 or more generations. I have known Bill now for 25 years. It has been his greatest concern that his own children and others will 'hang onto' this knowledge, this wisdom.

Bill is on about attitudes and values. The future rests on ours.

ALLAN FOX

Rock stays,
earth stays.

I die and put my bones in cave or earth.
Soon my bones become earth,
all the same.

My spirit has gone back to my country,
my mother.

Dreaming place,
you can't change it,
no matter who you are.
No matter you rich man,
no matter you king.
You can't change it.

I feel it with my body,
with my blood.
Feeling all these trees,
all this country.
When this wind blow you can feel it.
Same for country,
You feel it.
You can look.
But feeling...
that make you.

Feeling make you.
Out there in open space,
he coming through your body.
Look while he blow and feel with your body,
because tree just about your brother or father
and tree is watching you.

Rotten tree.
You got to burn him.
Use him to cook,
He's finished up.
Cook or roast in coals.
White European cook in oven,
from university that.
Aborigine didn't know that before.
Now all this coming up with Toyota.

This earth
I never damage.
I look after.
Fire is nothing,
just clean up.
When you burn,
new grass coming up.

Barramundi good in the wet season,
still good after the wet because of rain.
Big barramundi from salt water.
He follow fresh water down river,
rain helping him.
He can make eggs.

We must get rain.
Law says we get rain.
He come along wet season
and go dry season.
Rain come down
and give us new fresh water.
Plants coming up new.
Yam, creeper. All plants new.
Then we get fruit, honey and things to live.

Tree, he change with rain.
He get new leaf,
he got to come because rain.

Yam he getting big too.

Tree.
He *watching you.*
You look at tree,
he listen to you.
He got no finger,
he can't speak.
But that leaf
he pumping, growing,
growing in the night.

While you sleeping
you dream something.
Tree and grass same thing.
They grow with your body,
with your feeling.

This ground never move.
I'll be buried here.
I'll be with my brother, my mother.
If I lose this,
where I'll be buried?
I'm hanging onto this ground.
I'll become earth again.
I belong to this earth.
And earth should stay with us.

Tree the same as me.
When he get old he'll die.
He'll be dead and burn.
He'll leave his ashes behind.
Tree become earth.

PERFECT
PASTA
at home

PERFECT
PASTA
at home

Bring Italy to your kitchen with over
80 quick and delicious recipes

PASTA
EVANGELISTS

SEVEN DIALS

CONTENTS

INTRODUCTION

First and foremost, *grazie* for picking up our book. We are Pasta Evangelists, a fresh pasta company based in London. We started the business back in 2016, delivering our first batch of freshly made gnocchi and basil pesto to friends. Fortunately, they liked it, word got out, and by the end of 2017 we were delivering boxes of our fresh pasta and sauces to a couple of hundred Londoners every week. A year later, Harrods was renovating its food hall and invited us to open our first fresh pasta concession there. We were a bit taken aback to be asked – we were barely a business! – but immensely proud. Of course we said yes, even though we knew nothing about retail, let alone in one of the world's most famous department stores. A few years on, our team is still there, and we take immense pleasure in serving (and talking about) pasta all day long.

Mainly, though, we're a pasta subscription company, offering boxes of freshly made pasta, authentic sauces and garnishes from Italy to our wonderful customers in all corners of the UK. At pastaevangelists.com, we have a menu of 15 different dishes each week, showcasing the wonderful and limitless world of pasta. In this book, we've included many of our favourite recipes, as well as some of the best-sellers from our website. We hope you'll enjoy making them and would love to hear from you – please do tag us on Facebook, Twitter or Instagram at @pastaevangelists.

Before you dive straight in, though, we want to tell you a bit about who we are and where we come from. Italian culture is full of stories and we are no different.

Roberta

One of our favourite recipes in this book, Orecchiette with Rocket and Potatoes (see page 176), is based on Roberta's memory of growing up in Puglia, a sun-drenched region of the Italian south. In this arid, sleepy outpost of the Italian peninsula, groves of ancient olive trees and white-washed buildings dominate the landscape. The soul of its people, meanwhile, is rooted in religion and family life. Little has changed here for centuries, and, for the Pugliese, this is no bad thing; tradition is everything.

It was 1989, and the young Roberta – then just six years old – was already causing her parents some concern. You see, of more than 20 children living on the d'Elia family farm, Roberta was the most rambunctious. Twice already she had been caught red-handed emerging from the tomato vines of her neighbour, Signorina Teresa. On the third such occasion, a red-faced Roberta (she had learned to devour her plunder there and then, rather than be encumbered during her retreat) was discovered in the vines not by Signorina Teresa but by Maria-Assunta, her nonna (grandmother) and head of the family. To the young Roberta, it did not seem of any consequence that, by pilfering tomatoes from the poor Signorina Teresa, she was defying her nonna's Catholic teachings. All that mattered in Roberta's mind were the sweet, blushing tomatoes, and how utterly wonderful they were.

For Maria-Assunta, though, a solution – or rather distraction – had to be found to keep her mischievous granddaughter occupied. To Roberta's delight, this entailed food, but on her grandmother's condition that it had to be fairly procured. And so, Roberta and her nonna began rising together before dawn, while the rest of the family slept, to explore the farmstead for anything they could forage. In those early days, this mainly meant *rucola* (rocket), which grows spontaneously across the d'Elia family's farmland. This herb, sprouting from the soil, was easy for Roberta to gather; still small, she could only look on as her nonna plucked olives, both green and black, from the land's centuries-old trees. By midday, when Puglia's searing heat set in, both grandmother and granddaughter would return to the cool of the farmhouse with baskets brimming with plenty of fresh *rucola*.

There, in the farmhouse kitchen, the real magic would begin. Roberta, by her own admission an impatient child, would watch, transfixed, as her nonna rolled out fresh pasta dough, shaping small pieces into orecchiette, or 'little ears', an iconic shape of Puglia (and one featured throughout this book). Maria-Assunta's orecchiette would be served for the entire family with the fresh rocket gathered earlier that morning, and with potatoes proffered by the men of the family, diced and boiled. This is where Roberta's favourite dish has its origins.

By 1991, after more than a year working by her nonna's side, Maria-Assunta anointed her granddaughter the family's pasta princess. To this day, Roberta credits the late Maria-Assunta with establishing her *Pugliesità* (the quality of being,

and feeling, Pugliese) through this formative time spent preparing orecchiette together in the farmhouse kitchen.

Alessandro

Around the same time, some 800 kilometres to the northwest, in the Italian Riviera, our co-founder Alessandro was also learning the virtues of pasta, albeit in a different milieu. Far from being confined to the *cucina* by his nonna's side, Alessandro – or Alex to those who know him well – was more often found terrorising the streets of his hometown, Genoa, with other teenage boys. He recalls being notorious among them for falling off his Aprilia scooter; one in five days are rainy there, and this climatic phenomenon, he insists, was responsible for the falls that so amused his friends. In any case, there was one weekly exception to this ritual, when Alex's loyalties lay elsewhere.

In Italy, schools open from Monday to Saturday, though they finish early – around 1pm. In this way, the weekend, as Alex and his friends knew it, began on Saturday afternoon. And as this weekly apotheosis came about, Alex would disappear off on his moped into the hills above the city. His friends, loitering in the *carrugi* (Genoa's historic narrow streets) below, could not comprehend this desertion. Like clockwork, when Alex rejoined the group the following morning, they would probe for a while, trying to tease out the reasons for his flight. But he'd never tell, and soon they'd let it go, only for the same thing to happen the next weekend.

The truth of Alex's whereabouts was known to only one other: his nonna, Maddalena. You see, while Alex had sat in lessons that morning, Maddalena had been preparing all of her grandson's favourite things to eat. This was not a proposition Alex could turn down, for Maddalena was a fantastic cook. Far less, though, could he tell a bunch of adolescent boys that he preferred spending time with Granny than them. And so, as his Aprilia lurched into his nonna's backstreet, he'd cast a glance over his shoulder before parking up. His friends never tailed him though; all he ever saw was the old town below and the Ligurian Sea in the distance. Secure in the knowledge that his Saturday secret was safe, Alex would announce *'nonna, sono qui!'* ('nonna, I'm here!'). As his nonna opened her home to her grandson, the smell of focaccia, baking in her oven, would fill the veranda. At this point, Alex's nose could discern which treats lay in store, and what level of rapture he might attain that afternoon.

Indeed, while focaccia is mainly understood outside of the region as being topped with olive oil, sea salt and perhaps rosemary, in Liguria varieties abound. Alex's favourite is *focaccia di recco*, made by sandwiching fresh stracchino cheese from the region between sheets of dough. If he was lucky, his nonna would have made this, and often she did. Most exciting for Alex, though, was watching Maddalena prepare her signature *gnocchi al pesto*. Just like Roberta, several hundred kilometres to the south, Alex would gaze on as his nonna rolled out the dough from flour, potato and eggs. She'd craft each individual gnocco by hand, using a *riga gnocchi*, a wooden board with ridges that give home-made gnocchi their rustic appearance. Once dragged gently down the board, each dumpling would be placed delicately on a floured surface before Maddalena moved onto the next. It was poignant to watch the hands of this wizened old woman move with such dexterity. The memory of these Saturday afternoon displays of craftsmanship would later provide Alex with the idea for Pasta Evangelists.

Finn

While all of this was happening, I (Finn) was little more than a big-bellied toddler on the other side of Europe, unable to compete with Roberta and Alex's early escapism through pasta. I grew up in the UK – in Newcastle upon Tyne, that proud, ferociously friendly bastion of the northeast, and though my childhood most certainly wasn't an Italian one (I ate more stotties than pasta), it *was* replete with delicious food.

My dad, Mark, had opened his first restaurant in the city a year before I was born. When it was reviewed with some favour in 1994 by a critic from *The Independent*, then a national broadsheet, I was barely a year old. The feature was quite an accolade for a Novocastrian restaurateur who had grown up on a council estate in the city's West End, son of a Polish immigrant. A critic coming 'all the way' from London had created quite the stir; the journalist even dedicated a couple of sentences to my existence, giving my parents a good telling off for letting their baby son play in the restaurant. My presence, she said, would upset diners, who would find the setting too familial. The reality, however, was that both of my parents worked full time and there was nowhere else for me to go. Yet I was glad to be there during my formative years, as my dad veered from one restaurant to another – it meant that I got to eat well (and often).

Looking back, many moments stand out for their gastronomic melodrama. The first involved me tasting a young pastry chef's new recipe in my dad's second restaurant. It was a blueberry butter cake, and it was so delicious that I requested three more to follow, devouring each in quick succession. By the end of the evening, I had eaten so much that I had to be carried, like some overfed pharoah in a palanquin, all the way home (at least three miles if my dad is to be believed). On another occasion – I think I was about nine – a gravy that my mother served with Sunday lunch delighted me so much that I literally wept. This has happened on a handful of occasions since, most recently at a pizzeria in West London, Pizzicotto. There, while battling a particularly grievous hangover, I was emotionally overcome by a Neapolitan-style pizza topped with a whole, fresh burrata and smatterings of basil pesto, served straight out of a 500°C wood-fired oven.

My lasting love affair with pasta *did* start in Italy, however, and merely became entrenched at Pasta Evangelists. I was visiting a family friend, Joanne, who was married to Marco, an Italian inventor. Marco had innovated a special stopper for vintage wine bottles and it was a great success. The two had since bought a beautiful villa by a small stream in the countryside near Venice. One evening, as the sun began to give way to shadow, Joanne and Marco invited me to their garden for dinner. As I sat at the table with the stream flowing by, my reverie was broken only by a mosquito biting at my ankle. The setting was otherwise so peaceful that I could have stayed there forever. After the preamble of *aperitivo* (see page 208), Joanne brought out the beef ragù she had been simmering for several hours beforehand. It was quite unlike anything I had ever tasted before, sumptuous and rich with fresh rosemary cut from the garden. Being a Brit, I devoured inordinate quantities of that ragù, each time with tangles of fresh tagliatelle from the local *pastificio* (little pasta factories). To the table, Marco explained that, in Italy, it is common to find family-owned *pastifici* that make and sell fresh pasta of exceptional quality. That evening in the Veneto countryside, with rosemary heady in the air, and red wine and ragù commingling in my belly, I remember really waking up to just how magnificent pasta *could* be.

Of course, like most Brits, I had grown up on dishes from the pseudo-Italian repertoire, notably spaghetti Bolognese. I now know that to Italians the notion of serving Bolognese sauce with spaghetti is tantamount to sacrilege. This sauce, they insist, must be served with tagliatelle. When Pasta Evangelists was born, and I began working and eating with Italians every day, I found these protestations difficult, even irritating. I thought them haughty, as though my Italian colleagues and friends were looking down their noses at us Brits. Who cares, I thought, if the sauce is served with tagliatelle, spaghetti or some other shape entirely for that matter?

What I have come to learn in the past few years, though, is that pasta means *something* to *everyone*, whether they are Italian, British, Chinese, Kenyan or Ecuadorian. It is a truly democratic food, one that transcends borders and is enjoyed in all corners of the world. In Italy, though, the meaning of pasta runs that bit deeper. It is an integral piece of this young nation's fabric, a matter of national pride and cohesion, uniting citizens from the sun-drenched island of Sicily in the Mediterranean, all the way up to Alpine communities in the far north. All Italians share a deep, personal stake in this precious foodstuff, and as we will see in this book, it is a vessel for the country's poetry, stories and history. Most importantly, pasta reminds Italians of precious years past, often when nonna was still lovingly present. So, today, when an Italian tells me that a pasta shape does, or perhaps does not, pair with some sauce, I listen. I listen even if their reaction seems unduly strong. I imagine for a second that, like Roberta, who spent years preparing orecchiette under the tutelage of her late nonna Maria-Assunta, the person protesting may have formed important memories of their own.

In these myriad ways, there is far more to pasta than meets the eye. That's why, as Pasta

Evangelists, we do all we can to evangelise this special food. By learning and telling the stories of pasta, we gain a far better understanding of it; in turn, this makes for a far more rewarding eating experience. By witnessing how real, fresh pasta is made from scratch, we appreciate this simple food more, understanding that its many permutations are the product of centuries of craftsmanship, creativity and artisan tradition. At the same time, we distinguish our pasta *evangelism* from puritanism – we do not, for example, insist there is no role for dried pasta, or that tradition must never be given a fresh outlook.

Instead, in this book, we've put together a selection of our favourite pasta recipes. Recipes that we, the Pasta Evangelists team, led by Alessandro, Finn and Roberta, enjoy in our homes in London. There are few, if any, restaurant techniques. The ingredients we use are, we hope, straightforward and easy to come by. Sometimes we make our own fresh pasta, sometimes we don't. On occasion, we find great joy in allowing a ragù to simmer for several hours. On others, we want something gratifyingly delicious to be ready in minutes. Whatever pasta promise you are hoping to fulfil, our objective is to help you make it happen in the most delicious of ways.

HOW TO USE THIS BOOK

We understand that, with the increasingly busy lives we all lead, there is less time for home cooking. At the same time, though, many of us are trying to eat more food that is fresh, delicious and unprocessed. This state of affairs – the desire to eat better food but with less time to prepare it – has helped make our Pasta Evangelists' subscription box so popular.

In this book, we have continued this ethos with a collection of delicious pasta recipes that can be made in under 30 minutes. We have also included a handful of special recipes, which take a little longer, and are perfect for those rare, but wonderful, periods of downtime, whether a long weekend or a break from work. There is also an assortment of 'make your own' dishes, inspired by the different regions of Italy. These provide ideas for how you can get creative using leftover ingredients and other bits and pieces for a very Italian 'fridge raid' experience.

Although we are principally a fresh pasta business, the recipes here have been designed to be served with dried pasta (and the weights we give are for dried pasta), as we appreciate this is widely available and not everyone is interested in making their own fresh pasta. Some people assume that dried pasta is somehow inferior to fresh pasta: this is not the case – they are simply two different products, and dried pasta will work well in all of the recipes featured in this book.

We do urge you to have a go at making your own fresh pasta, though. It's far simpler than many assume, and takes very little time and effort. To that end, we've also included a section showing you how to make your own pasta dough (traditional egg dough, and even vegan pasta dough) as well as the seven simple shapes used throughout the book.

Happy cooking and *buon appetito*.

A PASTAIA'S PANTRY

A note from Roberta

Ciao ragazzi. I'm Roberta, head *pastaia* and *sfoglina* at Pasta Evangelists. These two Italian words mean more or less the same thing: a person who makes pasta, like me. The only difference is that a *sfoglina* is typically a lady, or *donna*, while a *pastaia* can just as easily be a *pastaio*, which is a male pasta chef. We *sfogline* (as the plural goes) have usually learned our craft directly from our *nonne*, or grandmothers, when we were little girls. To this day, I use the knife passed down to me by my own *nonna*, Maria-Assunta, who sadly is no longer with us but will forever be in my heart (as well as in my conscience in the kitchen and beyond!).

I come from Puglia, in the southeast of Italy, a very traditional region where Catholicism remains influential. I grew up on a farm, on the outskirts of a city called Foggia, with 20 or so other family members. Our cuisine comes from a tradition called *cucina povera*, meaning 'the poor man's kitchen'. We have always been an impoverished region and rely on simple, inexpensive ingredients to sustain us. My favourite pasta shape, orecchiette (meaning 'little ears'), for example, is a *pasta bianca*, made without any egg. This is because, for centuries, eggs were an unaffordable luxury in my region. They're easier to come by today, of course, but the tradition remains in our hearts.

In this section, I've included some of my top tips when preparing pasta dishes – from which eggs and salt to use to how long to cook pasta for.

I hope you will find the information useful. If you haven't yet tried making your own fresh pasta to go with the sauces in this book, I urge you to try it. It's a lot easier than it sounds (I promise) and is a fantastic upper body workout . . . or so I tell myself, anyway!

From my kitchen to yours, happy cooking and *buon appetito*.

COOKING PASTA

For the recipes in this book, I've given the weights for *pasta secca*, or dried pasta. Because dried pasta expands during cooking, you need less of it than you would fresh pasta. In Italy, where pasta is normally served as a *primo*, or starter, the rule is 100g of dried or 165g of fresh pasta per person. In the UK, where I've learned pasta is more widely enjoyed as a standalone dish, I allow for 125g of dried or 200g of fresh pasta per person. Of course, you can always dial down the quantity of pasta used if you're serving it alongside other dishes.

Here are five helpful tips for preparing pasta at home:
1. Use 1 litre of water per 100g of dried pasta. All too often I see people trying to squeeze vast amounts of pasta into a tiny pan with a scant amount of water. The pasta requires space to cook and expand and is likely to stick if you don't cook it in a big enough pan with plenty of water.

2. It's essential to properly salt pasta water. There's an old saying in Italy that the water should be as salty as our Mediterranean Sea, and that's true. I recommend 10g of coarse sea salt per litre of water. This may seem like a lot, but only a tiny amount of it is absorbed by the pasta during cooking. Undersalting the pasta cooking water is one of the key reasons a pasta dish can end up bland, so don't skimp on salt.

3. Only add the pasta to the water once it has been salted and has reached a ferocious boil.

4. Follow packet instructions for cooking times, but try a piece of pasta a minute or two before the end of cooking to see if it's done. In Italy, we like our pasta 'al dente', meaning 'to the teeth' – this basically means that the pasta continues to have a bit of bite and hasn't become too soft.

5. If you have made your own fresh pasta, most shapes take just 1–2 minutes to cook. Fresh pasta can also be frozen for a month or so and cooked straight from frozen, allowing an extra minute or so of cooking time.

DRIED PASTA

Dried pasta is more common in the Italian south, where, for generations, the eggs used to prepare fresh pasta were an unaffordable luxury. Today, although eggs are more widely available in the south, old habits die hard. And it isn't the case that fresh is better than dried, or vice versa; they're simply different things.

If you have dried pasta to hand, there is undoubtedly a potential meal to be had, no matter how sparse your cupboard may be. This book contains 80 recipes that put dried pasta to use in different ways, and a good many of them require just a handful of store cupboard staples.

Pasta can be served as simply as in *pasta aglio e olio*, which is pasta with garlic fried until fragrant in olive oil. Ultimately, the key is to pick a high-quality pasta – my favourite brand is De Cecco, with the beautiful blue and yellow packets that you can't miss, but you can also look for any pasta with the words 'di Gragnano' on the packet. Gragnano pasta, named after a town on the Amalfi Coast, is made with a special bronze dye that gives each piece a rustic finish. This, in turn, allows sauces to properly cling to the pasta, resulting in a more satisfying eating experience.

I should also say that a lot of people think all dried pasta is the same, just branded and packaged differently, a bit like paracetamol tablets. This isn't the case, though: pasta is similar to bread, with different production methods and finishes. As even the best types of dried pasta are relatively affordable, I recommend going for the highest quality varieties where you can.

FRESH PASTA

Fresh pasta is more widely enjoyed in the north of Italy, particularly in cities like Bologna, where tagliatelle is freshly made and served with rich, meat-based sauces known as ragùs. In Italy – again, especially in the north – you are able to visit *pastifici* to buy fresh pasta. These are little pasta factories, usually family-run, that produce small batches of fresh pasta every day for their customers. Unfortunately, no such equivalent exists here in the UK, which is why we set up Pasta Evangelists: to bring the joy of really fresh, artisan pasta to homes across the country.

People often tell us that they can buy fresh pasta at the supermarket, which isn't strictly true. Pick up a packet of 'fresh' pasta in the supermarket the next time you're there, and have a look at the best before date: chances are, the pasta will have an expiry date one or two months in the future. We always find this puzzling, because no other fresh ingredient, whether herbs, salad leaves or tomatoes, lasts anywhere near as long. The reason supermarket fresh pasta does so is because it is highly pasteurised and often contains lots of preservatives. We don't recommend buying or eating it, not only for these reasons but because it is incomparable to real fresh pasta. If you can, have a go at making your own (see page 214); if not, quality dried pasta is always the better option.

SALT

Always ensure a sauce contains enough salt before serving. Salt, or *sale* as we call it in Italy, has a fantastic ability to bring out the flavour of other ingredients when used correctly. As Italian food is generally quite simple, with only a handful of ingredients, adding too little salt to a recipe is one of the most frequent reasons a dish can be bland.

Salt is also useful in lots of other ways. For example, when I'm preparing a fresh tomato sauce in a pan, I always add salt right after the tomatoes, as it helps the tomatoes break down and create a liquid base. If I'm too lazy to peel the tomatoes before adding them to the pan (which is often the case), the salt is particularly important to help the skins of the tomatoes split and disintegrate. In a similar way, adding salt to the flesh of watery vegetables like courgettes, aubergines or mushrooms can help draw out excess water prior to cooking.

In the UK, my favourite brand of sea salt for seasoning dishes and sauces is Maldon Sea Salt. You can use virtually any type of salt for pasta water – the key is simply to ensure the water is salty enough.

EGGS

When I lived in Puglia, my favourite walk was to an old neighbour, Signor Carmine, who had his own brood of hens. He insisted I go into the coop myself to retrieve the eggs. I was terrified of his hens, and so the memory is difficult to erase, but it was arguably worth it. The freshness of the eggs and their beautiful orange yolks was beyond comparison. Sadly, it's often assumed eggs are much of a muchness, but this isn't so.

A carbonara sauce, for example, can live or die based on the quality of the eggs used, because there are so few other ingredients to hide behind. The key is to use the freshest eggs you can, ideally only a day or two after they have been laid. I appreciate this is a challenge in cities, but you'll often be able to find fresh eggs at farmers' markets. The next best bet is to use the wonderful Burford Brown variety from our friends at Clarence Court, which are now widely stocked in supermarkets. Their golden yolks are completely sublime, making them perfect for making pasta too, as the colour of the yolk determines the colour of the pasta.

FLOUR

Like eggs and dried pasta, flour (*farina* in Italian), is often thought of as a simple ingredient with little real difference between the numerous varieties stocked on supermarket shelves. This is not the case, and different types of flour serve different purposes.

In the Italian tradition, for example, *doppio zero* or 00 flour is almost exclusively used for pasta-making; few nonne, for example, would countenance the use of plain white flour, for it isn't fine enough in consistency. 00 flour, on the other hand, is the finest flour produced, making it easy to roll out into the thinnest possible sheets of dough without these breaking. This, in turn, enables pasta chefs to produce, say, ravioli with beautifully light encasings, allowing the filling to shine through without the stodginess of the pasta getting in the way. Other egg pasta shapes, usually from the north, are also made from oo flour, including Bologna's tagliatelle and Tuscany's hearty pappardelle. Nowadays, you can buy oo flour in almost all of the big supermarkets, so it's easy to find and experiment with.

In the south of Italy, the most common flour in the pantry is likely *semola di grano duro*. This should not be confused with semolina, which is an entirely different ingredient. Semola is made from hard wheat, and is a largely unrefined product with an intense yellow colour from the coarse grains it's made from. It's used to prepare *pasta bianca*, or white pasta, made without eggs. Shapes including my favourite orecchiette, as well as malloreddus and cavatelli, are made using this type of flour. In the UK, I buy my semola online; my favourite brand is Divella.

CHEESE

Parmigiano-Reggiano, known as Parmesan in the UK, is one of the protagonists of Italian cuisine. This is true all across the country, despite this cheese originating in the town of Parma in Emilia-Romagna. It has a fantastically tangy, salty flavour and takes on more intensity as it ages. Most varieties you'll find in the UK have been aged for 12 to 24 months, but it's not uncommon in Italy to find varieties aged for 36 months or longer. I'm often asked at our pasta masterclasses if Parmesan is suitable during pregnancy, and can gladly confirm it is; because it contains very little water compared to soft cheeses, it isn't hospitable to bacteria. This also means it can be kept for quite some time, so I always have a good amount of it stashed away in the store cupboard (aside from flour it's the only ingredient I never run out of!).

Do experiment with other cheeses too, though. Italy is home to countless wonderful varieties and each has its own character. After Parmesan, my second favourite cheese is pecorino Romano, which is a sheep's cheese with a moderately strong, salty flavour.

Throughout this book, I've included the words 'or vegetarian alternative' after several of the cheeses listed in the ingredients. This is because many cheeses, such as Parmigiano-Reggiano, are unsuitable for vegetarians owing to the use of rennet, made from enzymes in cows' stomachs. Fortunately, a wide variety of vegetarian alternatives can be found – however, due to European law, these alternatives can't have the same name as the cheese they're emulating. So for a vegetarian substitute for Parmesan, for example, you'll have to look out for what is often branded 'Vegetarian Italian Hard Cheese'. For all intents and purposes, it tastes exactly the same as Parmigiano-Reggiano and can be substituted with confidence.

TOMATOES

When I was growing up in Puglia, the end of summer was marked by what we call the *passata di pomodori*, or last of the tomatoes. This was always in August. Under my nonna's supervision, we would harvest the sweetest of the tomatoes one last time, working as a family out in the sun, peeling and boiling them in a ginormous pot over firewood for hours at a time. The smell of the fresh tomatoes in the August sun, with cicadas chirping in the background, is, for me, the memory of *la famiglia* and carefree years gone by. Many Italians from the south will be able to relate. After hours of work, we'd have countless jars of tomato sauce that we could stow away and use during the rest of the year when tomatoes were no longer in season.

Now, 20 years on and living in the UK, I have the supreme good fortune to continue to be sent fresh passata from my family's farm for use during the cold winter months. Although modern farming practices and globalisation mean tomatoes are available in British supermarkets year round, I find them inedible outside of the summer months. They seem to lack all flavour and resemble big red water balloons. For this reason, I advise against using fresh tomatoes to prepare recipes in this book outside of summer. The best brand of tinned tomatoes to be used at other times during the year is, in my opinion, Mutti. And during the promising summer months, take time to select the best tomatoes you can: look for blushing red skins, vivid green vines and a strong, sweet aroma.

OLIVE OIL

Few ingredients remind me of home quite so much as extra virgin olive oil. The area I grew up in was surrounded by olive groves, so many in fact that the street my father lives on is called Via Deglia Ulivi (Olive Tree Street). At the end of October, my whole family would rally round to harvest the olive crop by hand. This is a physically demanding and onerous process but it yields by far the best olives when compared with mechanical production, for harvesting by hand allows you to discard inferior olives as you go and avoid damaging the delicate fruit with electric machinery. We'd collect the olives in a basket, or drop them into nets surrounding the trees, and take them to the nearest *frantaio*, or olive oil press. I remember the strong, unpleasant smell of the

olives as a little girl, but the cascade of their oil (which we call 'liquid gold') that poured from the press was enchanting. Bruschetta doused in the freshly pressed oil was a ritual after these trips and marked the end of the harvest.

Fortunately, as olive oil is widely exported, fantastic varieties can be found here in the UK. Unfortunately, there are just as many of poor quality that should be avoided. As a general rule, try to avoid bottles that feature the words 'by mechanical means' on the label. I get all my olive oil from The Olive Oil Co., which has stalls at Broadway and Borough Markets in London, but also a fantastic online store for those living further afield (you may have to drop them an email to order, but they'll be remarkably helpful and thankful for your custom). I like the 'Tre Foglie' variety, which is from my home region and tastes fantastic.

ANCHOVIES

I know not everyone likes the idea of anchovies, but they are a true staple in my store cupboard. They have a unique way of adding deep savoury notes to all manner of dishes and can be 'melted' down in hot oil so you don't even know they're there. I use anchovies in my Working Girl's Spaghetti (see page 77) and Seafarer's Spaghetti (see page 116), and so always have some to hand. Choose a variety preserved in extra virgin olive oil without any added aromatics. And glass packaging is better than metal cases as you can see what you are buying.

NUTS

Nuts are a key ingredient in the Mediterranean diet, and are cultivated widely across Italy, with the best pistachios coming from Bronte in Sicily, and walnuts from Sorrento. We use all manner of nuts in my country, from almonds and pine nuts to walnuts and hazelnuts. In this book, they're the base of several different pestos. I particularly like blanched (white, skinless) almonds in pesto for the way they add creaminess. Because they don't perish particularly quickly, I recommend keeping a wide assortment of nuts in your store cupboard. They're incredibly good for you too.

LEGUMES

Pulses provide a fantastic source of protein and are a cheaper and more environmentally friendly alternative to meat-based sauces. For this reason, they've been a staple in my region's *cucina povera* for centuries (if not millennia) and a source of nutrition for peasants on the Italian peninsula through the ages.

I particularly like lentils, which I use to create a vegetarian ragù (see page 182). The best and most economical way to consume pulses is to buy dried and cook them at home as required. This can take some time, with soaking required the night before, so it's often worth having a couple of cans of precooked beans, chickpeas and lentils on hand for emergencies, too.

GARLIC, ONION, CARROTS AND CELERY

This may seem like an odd grouping, but these ingredients combine when gently fried in olive oil to form a *soffritto*, which is the base of many sauces (particularly meat-based) in this book.

In some recipes, you'll see only garlic. Most of the time, I simply peel a garlic clove and fry it whole in olive oil, then discard it. This infuses the oil with the fragrance and taste of garlic without leaving large, acrid pieces behind. In recipes where the garlic is left in the pan, or minced into the sauce, take real care not to burn it when you're frying it; the oil should never be too hot when you add the garlic and, if it does burn, it's best to start over rather than proceed with a burnt base, as this will compromise the whole dish. The same goes for onion, though this is less likely to burn unless subject to truly ferocious heat.

HERBS

Fresh herbs are used widely in Italian cuisine, and I recommend maintaining a little herb garden of your own for the sake of convenience. I grow fresh basil, parsley and thyme on my kitchen windowsill, with rosemary and sage growing just outside in the garden. You'd be surprised how many herbs can prosper indoors with relatively little attention; you can even buy them ready-potted from the supermarket and leave them sitting on a saucer, pouring water directly onto the saucer so the herbs can absorb it as they need it. Be careful of them bolting, however – particularly basil. This is when they begin to produce flowers at the end of the lifecycle and their flavour diminishes considerably; it's worth plucking off a leaf and having a little nibble before committing a handful to a recipe. If you are decidedly not green-fingered, however, all of the fresh herbs used in this book can be found prepacked in supermarkets.

I don't use dried herbs as often in my recipes, though they are important in some places. Dried oregano, in particular, is a good herb to keep stocked in the pantry.

ITALY: A Story of 20 Regions

IF THERE'S ONE THING YOU SHOULD KNOW ABOUT ITALY, it's that it's a young country. This might seem a strange thing to say. After all, the Italian capital, Rome, was once the centre of an ancient empire stretching from North Africa in the south all the way to the border between England and Scotland in the north. Even today, echoes of the Roman Empire continue to dominate the 'Eternal City', as Rome is nicknamed for its virtually timeless history and amaranthine beauty. Its imposing Colosseum, a symbol of Western civilisation, was built between 70 and 80 AD and towers over Rome's streets, reminding us of the city's millennia of history. That the city was also named *Caput Mundi* (capital of the world) in Latin, however also tells us of Rome's cosmopolitan nature.

The story of Rome, then, is really the story of the Western world. It encompasses the Iberian peninsula (comprising Spain and Portugal, and known in Latin as Hispania) as much as it does the Italian peninsula or any of the Roman Empire's countless provinces spread across the Mediterranean and Western Asia for that matter. What, then, is the story of *Italy*?

In the nineteenth century, a movement known as the *Risorgimento* ('resurgence') saw multiple independent states spread across the Italian peninsula come together to form the Kingdom of Italy, the precursor to today's Italian Republic. Until Rome was made the capital of the new country in 1871, there was no Italy per se; only a scattered selection of smaller countries that themselves drifted in and out of history.

The Republic of Venice, for example, existed for over a millennium, becoming a major maritime power in its own right before being gobbled up by the Austrian Empire at the turn of the eighteenth century. The Aperol spritz (see Aperitivo, page xx) is, to this day, seen as much in the Austrian capital Vienna as it is in any city of modern Italy. Rome, meanwhile, was the capital of an altogether different country, the Papal States, ruled from the Eternal City by the Pope.

Separated from the Italian peninsula by the Mediterranean, the island of Sicily had its own chequered history, even being ruled by Arabs as the Islamic Emirate of Sicily for more than 200 years. Visitors to the island's capital, Palermo, are often struck by the elaborate arabesque decorations on the walls of its structures, reminding us of the island's many different rulers from exotic places. By the time Arab rule in Sicily ended in 1091, England, by way of comparison, had been a unified country for more than a century. Italy as we know it was still nowhere to be seen, nor would it be for another seven centuries.

In this respect, Italy is not merely a new nation, but an incredibly diverse one. In England, a 'north–south divide' is often described, documenting the different levels of productivity, cultures and dialects found across the country. Geordies like Finn, for example, often feel they come from an altogether different country to those growing up in, say, the Home Counties surrounding London. After more than a millennium of national unity, England remains diverse within its own borders. The diversity of Italy, then, with less than two centuries of national unity, cannot be emphasised enough.

Italy is not merely a new nation, but an incredibly diverse one

Within Italy's modest territory of a little over 300,000 square kilometres, you'll find countless different languages and vernaculars, striking geographical differences and, of course, distinct regional gastronomies. Sardu, the language of more than a million people on the Italian island of Sardinia, for example, is deemed to be as easy for Italian speakers to understand as French! Meanwhile, many Italians from the north's Alpine regions will never have seen a volcano, while for the three million people living in Naples, the backdrop of nearby Mount Vesuvius is a daily vista. Unlike Neapolitans, the people of Parma in Emilia-Romagna to the north need not worry that their hometown might one day be buried under volcanic ash as Pompeii once was. And with Parmigiano-Reggiano and prosciutto di Parma both hailing from the town, they arguably lead far better lives. Neapolitans would disagree, however, in spite of the volcano's threat, citing the beauty of the Bay of Naples or the wonders of their eponymous pizza.

Sadly, Italians are also divided along economic lines. The eight regions of the Italian north, blessed by geography with greater proximity to other European countries, were the first to reap the benefits of industrialisation, becoming wealthier than the south, as they remain. The 12 southern regions, meanwhile, were left behind, remaining largely agrarian communities. In 2018, the percentage of the population of Sicily at risk of poverty stood at more than 40 per cent. In the region of Friuli-Venezia Giulia, on the other side of the country, the rate was five times lower.

But it isn't all bad news for the south, which has become rich in altogether different ways. In Italy, the word *mezzogiorno*, literally 'midday', also describes the southern regions. This is quite bizarre for non-native speakers, who are puzzled to hear an entire half of the Italian peninsula referred to by the name 'midday' in weather forecasts. In true Italian style, there is a certain poetry to this: the south is called *mezzogiorno* because, at midday in Italy, the bright sun shines from the south. And while some southerners might feel that sunshine is an unfitting, perhaps even insulting, allegory for their downtrodden regions, we are deeply enchanted by them, and not only because Roberta comes from the region of Puglia in the southern half of the peninsula.

That's why, throughout this book, you'll see little nods to the Italian south, whether in the frequent use of fresh red chillies, widely added to recipes in the sun-drenched south and less so in the northern regions, or our enthusiasm for southern pasta shapes like orecchiette and malloreddus, both made without egg. These habits, part of a wider culture in the south known as *cucina povera*, or 'poor man's kitchen', tell us real Italian stories. Eggs, for example, are left out of most of the south's fresh pasta because they were – and often remain – an unaffordable luxury. This results in *pasta bianca*, or 'white pasta' (for it lacks the golden glow afforded by egg yolks), being strongly associated with the region. In the affluent northeastern region of Veneto, a local pasta shape known as bigoli is often made not merely with hen's eggs but expensive duck eggs, too. This would seem unthinkably indulgent in southern regions like Campania or Calabria, underlining the fact that differences in gastronomy are rooted less in different tastes and more in economy and everyday means.

Eggs, are left out of most of the south's fresh pasta because they were — and often remain — an unaffordable luxury.

Of course, our appreciation for the Italian south comes not at the expense of the north. Regions from Piedmont and Liguria in the northwest to Veneto and Emilia-Romagna in the northeast, have bestowed edible treasures of their own on Italian cuisine, and many feature in this book. It also goes without saying that the particular treasures of the Tuscan kitchen – take pappardelle, cavolo nero and wild boar ragù (see page 206) – make Italian cuisine an altogether richer experience. It's also worth remembering that many northern dishes also have peasant origins, and should not be dismissed as decadent by design.

In any case, our ambition in this book is to whisk you away, wherever you might be, for a real taste of Italy in your own home. We want to show you the sheer variety that can be found in the fabric of modern Italy. With 20 regions, each with its own distinct cuisine and many their own language entirely, there is so much to see, touch, smell, hear and taste. This book will only be able to scratch the surface of this special place, but we hope you'll find the stories of the country we both know and love to be interesting and informative and the recipes delicious.

PART 1

10 MINUTES

There's some tacit understanding that recipes that are quick to prepare are somehow inferior; that they inevitably give less joy or are less impressive than food laboured over for many hours. If you haven't toiled over a hot stove for the whole day before your guests arrive, you question whether you have made enough effort. This outlook is particularly grounded in our fast-food world, where rapidly prepared food tends to be synonymous with processed ingredients and cheat techniques. Fortunately, as generations of Italians have understood, it doesn't need to be this way.

All the recipes in this section can be made within 10 minutes, though not because of any wizardry or kitchen chicanery. We see no way, for example, that a tough cut of beef shin might be slow-cooked to perfection in a matter of minutes, and so we don't recommend 'cheat' techniques as others may do. Instead, the ingredients used in these recipes simply don't require much, if any, cooking.

When you have high-quality, fresh produce to hand, it often pays to keep things simple and let the natural flavours and textures of the ingredients shine. It is in quick dishes of this sort that we can take the greatest advantage of bright flavours that haven't been dulled by the cooking process. Lemon zest, pancetta, fresh herbs and delicate cheeses all spring to mind here.

Take the Broad Bean Pesto (see page 48), which is a staple in many kitchens of the Italian Riviera. This sauce requires only a handful of easily sourced ingredients, straight from the pantry and fridge. Pounded together in a matter of moments, the result is a fresh, vibrant sauce with flavours unadulterated by cooking. Better still, as with many recipes in this section, it can be prepared while the pasta is boiling.

Spaghetti with the carbonara of dreams

SPAGHETTI ALLA CARBONARA

serves 4

When we photographed this dish, our photographer Tim exclaimed that he was shooting the 'Carbonara of Dreams'. If you ask Tim why he christened it so, we hope he'd say it's because this carbonara has a way of whisking you away from your worldly troubles, if only for a moment, which we've invariably found is as long as a bowl of this pasta lasts.

For the people of Lazio, and especially the capital Rome, two rules should be observed when preparing this dish. First, the addition of cream is aberrant. Second, the pork component should be guanciale, a fatty, cured cut from a pig's cheek. That is to say, in the Roman view, lardons or smoked bacon are not to be substituted. In respect of tradition, we therefore give you Roberta's carbonara recipe as you'd find it in the Italian capital.

500g spaghetti
150g guanciale (if you really can't find it, opt for cubed pancetta)
5 medium egg yolks
50g pecorino Romano, grated, plus extra to serve
Salt and black pepper, to taste

1. Bring a pot of generously salted water to the boil. Cook the pasta until al dente, following the packet instructions. While the pasta cooks, prepare the sauce.
2. Remove and discard the tough rind of the guanciale, then cut the meat into cubes. Place the cubes in a cold, dry frying pan over a low heat and cook for 5–6 minutes until crisp and browned, then remove from the heat.
3. While the guanciale cooks, place the egg yolks in a bowl (Roberta recommends saving the egg whites for an omelette). Add the pecorino, salt and pepper, and beat with a fork until combined.
4. Once the pasta is al dente, reserve a cup of the starchy pasta cooking water, then drain the pasta and add it to the pan containing the guanciale. Return the pan to a low heat and sauté the pasta for a few minutes, adding a splash of the cooking water.
5. Remove the pan from the heat and add the egg yolk mixture. Toss the pasta in the sauce continuously, adding more cooking water if necessary. You should be left with a glossy sauce that completely coats the spaghetti.
6. Plate and serve immediately with freshly grated pecorino Romano and black pepper to taste.

Orecchiette with fresh tomato & stracciatella

V/Ve

ORECCHIETTE AL POMODORO FRESCO E STRACCIATELLA   *serves 4*

Roberta reckons this might be her favourite pasta dish of all. For her, it symbolises everything beautiful about her home region of Puglia. There, tomatoes grow locally and are fantastically sweet and fragrant. Orecchiette, her beloved pasta shape, are made by hand by nonne throughout the region, and remain an enduring symbol of Pugliese pride. Stracciatella, a fresh cheese from her hometown of Foggia, is made with the milk of Italian buffaloes, which graze throughout the region, and can be bought from local cheesemakers.

The key here, as is often the case in the Italian kitchen, is selecting ingredients of the highest possible quality. Stracciatella can be a little difficult to come by, but it is available at most Italian delis. If you can't find it, you may be able to find burrata, whose oozing core is composed of stracciatella. Failing that, quality *mozzarella di bufala* will work well too.

500g orecchiette

*5 tbsp extra virgin olive oil,
    plus extra to serve*

*1 garlic clove, peeled and lightly
    crushed*

*15–20g fresh basil leaves, shredded,
    plus extra to serve*

*400g fresh tomatoes, washed
    and diced*

2 tsp sea salt flakes

120g fresh stracciatella

1. Bring a pot of generously salted water to the boil. Cook the pasta until al dente, following the packet instructions. While the pasta cooks, prepare the sauce.
2. Heat the oil in a pan over a medium heat. Add the garlic and sauté for 2 minutes until fragrant. When the garlic turns golden brown, remove from the pan and discard.
3. Add the basil leaves to the pan. Take care here, as the oil may spit. Allow the basil to infuse in the oil for 30 seconds, then add the tomatoes and sea salt flakes. Stir until well combined, then cover and cook for 5–6 minutes until the sauce is thick and glossy.
4. Once the pasta is al dente, drain the pasta and add it to the pan containing the tomato sauce, tossing it in the sauce until coated.
5. Plate and serve immediately, topped with the stracciatella cheese, as well as extra basil and a drizzle of extra virgin olive oil.

Spaghetti from the Amalfi Coast

SPAGHETTI AL LIMONE

V/Ve

serves 4

Sixty kilometres or so south of Naples lies the Costiera Amalfitana, or Amalfi Coast. Its Italian name is a portmanteau of Amalfi and Positano, two towns set on cliffs along the seafront. In this special place, pastel structures line the streets and local fishermen can be seen going about their business. Most of all, though, Amalfi is known for its eponymous lemons, which grow abundantly along the sun-kissed coastline. Amalfi lemons are distinguished by their unusually large size and sweet, perfumed flavour, and whenever we visit, we love to eat *pasta al limone*: a simple, gorgeously fragrant sauce made with these special lemons. This is our version, best enjoyed with a glass of chilled white wine in the late afternoon sun (like just about all things in life).

500g spaghetti
2 tbsp olive oil
20g unsalted butter
1 garlic clove, peeled and lightly crushed
400ml single cream
Juice and grated zest of 2 unwaxed lemons
Salt and black pepper, to taste
Parmesan, or vegetarian alternative, to serve

1. Bring a pot of generously salted water to the boil. Cook the pasta until al dente, following the packet instructions. While the pasta cooks, prepare the sauce.

2. Place the oil and butter in a large pan over a medium heat. When the butter has melted, add the garlic and fry gently for around 2 minutes until golden. Once the oil mixture is fragrant, take the pan off the heat and discard the garlic clove. Slowly add the cream and stir to combine. Return the pan to a low heat and continue to stir gently until the sauce begins to bubble.

3. Remove from the heat again, then add the lemon juice and zest, salt and pepper.

4. Once the pasta is al dente, reserve a cup of the starchy pasta cooking water, then drain the pasta and add it to the pan containing the sauce. Stir over a low heat to combine, adding a splash of the cooking water if necessary, to obtain a glossy sauce which completely coats the pasta.

5. Plate and serve immediately with freshly grated Parmesan to taste.

Gnocchi with truffle butter

GNOCCHI AL TARTUFO

V/Ve

serves 4

By most accounts, Italy is the world's second largest producer of truffles after China. This doesn't surprise us, because the Italian appetite for truffles – *tartufi* – is substantial. This is particularly so in the northern and central regions where restaurants often serve specialities such as truffle and potato ravioli. In fact, truffles have a near mythical status in some parts of the country, and it is commonly said that they are snuffled out by pigs. Nowadays, this work is almost exclusively undertaken by dogs since pigs refuse to give up the truffles they unearth and devour them instead. Quite understandable, we think.

500g gnocchi

120g unsalted butter

60g black or white truffle, shaved or finely grated (or a mixture of the two); set aside some shavings to serve

Salt, to taste

Parmesan, or vegetarian alternative, to serve

1. Cook the gnocchi, following the packet instructions. While the gnocchi cook, prepare the sauce.
2. Melt the butter in a large frying pan. Add the truffle and stir to combine, then add salt to taste. Take the pan off the heat and let the truffle infuse in the butter.
3. Add the cooked gnocchi to the truffle butter, tossing the mixture until the dumplings are completely coated.
4. Plate and serve immediately, topped with the extra truffle shavings and freshly grated Parmesan to taste.

'Greek' Rigatoni

RIGATONI ALLA GRICIA

serves 4

This dish is shrouded in mystery. Essentially a carbonara without the addition of egg, *Pasta alla Gricia* literally means 'pasta in the manner of the Greeks'. This is odd, given its constituent elements are all decidedly Italian (particularly guanciale, a cured cut from a pig's cheek). *Pasta alla Gricia* is also a bona fide Roman dish: veritably ancient, the dish has been prepared on the Italian peninsula since at least 400 AD. While many theories have been proffered to explain how this dish ended up invoking the Greeks, we think it likely that the confusion stems from a simple spelling mistake: the town of Grisciano, just 15 kilometres from Amatrice, is probably the true home of the dish.

500g rigatoni

300g guanciale (if you really can't find it, opt for cubed pancetta)

70g pecorino Romano, grated, plus extra to serve

1. Bring a pot of generously salted water to the boil. Cook the pasta until al dente, following the packet instructions. While the pasta cooks, prepare the sauce.

2. Remove and discard the tough rind of the guanciale, then cut the meat into cubes. Place the cubes in a dry frying pan over a medium-high heat, moving the meat constantly to ensure it doesn't burn. Allow the guanciale to brown in the rendered fat for 6–7 minutes.

3. Once the pasta is al dente, reserve a cup of the starchy pasta cooking water, then drain the pasta and add it to the pan with the guanciale. Reduce the heat to low and sauté the pasta for a few minutes, adding a splash of cooking water. Toss until the pasta is completely coated in the glossy sauce.

4. Add the pecorino Romano and combine until the cheese is incorporated.

5. Plate and serve immediately with freshly grated pecorino Romano to taste.

Finn's green yoghurt pasta

Finn loves Middle Eastern ingredients and was enraptured to find a recipe for pasta with yoghurt in Yotam Ottolenghi's classic cookbook *Jerusalem*. He knew, though, that Roberta was unlikely to allow the idea of feta or Aleppo chilli with pasta, but imagined that, with some tweaks, she might just tolerate the yoghurt element. As it happened, he needn't have worried: she loves it.

Finn substituted ricotta salata for the feta, which is eminently Italian and has a similar, if slightly less prominent, degree of saltiness. The Aleppo pepper vanished too, replaced with peperoncino (chilli) flakes. Finn also likes lots of spinach here, not because it's Italian per se, but rather because it gives the sauce a wonderful green colour. The spinach also seems to have an absolving property, making you feel better in body and soul if you've had a heavy night the day before devouring this. And by his own admission, Finn often has.

500g orecchiette

75g spinach, washed

1 garlic clove, peeled

125g full-fat Greek yoghurt

2 tbsp extra virgin olive oil,
plus extra to serve

½ tsp sea salt flakes

30g fresh basil leaves

100g peas, fresh or frozen
and defrosted

½ tsp dried red chilli flakes

Juice of 1 lemon

100g ricotta salata, crumbled

1. Bring a pot of generously salted water to the boil. Cook the pasta until al dente, following the packet instructions. While the pasta cooks, prepare the sauce.

2. Blitz the spinach, garlic, yoghurt, olive oil and sea salt flakes in a blender with half the fresh basil leaves, half the peas and half the dried red chilli flakes. Once blitzed, stir through the lemon juice and set aside.

3. A minute before the pasta is done, add the remaining peas to the boiling water and finish cooking. Drain the pasta and peas and return to the pan.

4. Pour the yoghurt sauce over the drained pasta and peas and stir to combine.

5. Roughly tear the remaining basil leaves and stir through the finished pasta along with the crumbled ricotta salata and the remaining red chilli flakes.

6. Plate and serve immediately, drizzled with extra virgin olive oil to complete the dish.

Rigatoni with ricotta

RIGATONI ALLA RICOTTA

serves 4

This recipe is a work of mere moments. With just a few ingredients, it also precludes any unwelcome spice searches or visits to specialist shops. Instead, the key ingredient, as the name suggests, is simply – but no less beautifully – ricotta, one of Italy's best-loved cheeses.

There are records of this special cheese being produced on the Italian peninsula as far back as the Bronze Age, meaning the tribes of early Italy have been gorging themselves on ricotta with great relish since before the days of Ancient Rome. We like to follow their example, albeit with a generous amount of seasoning and a good grating of Parmesan to offset the subtle sweetness of the ricotta.

500g rigatoni

400g ricotta

1–2 sprigs of fresh thyme, leaves removed from the stem

Parmesan, or vegetarian alternative, grated, plus extra to serve

Salt and black pepper, to taste

1. Bring a pot of generously salted water to the boil. Cook the pasta until al dente, following the packet instructions. While the pasta cooks, prepare the sauce.
2. In a large bowl, combine the ricotta with some fresh thyme leaves, salt, pepper and a little grated Parmesan, if desired.
3. Once the pasta is al dente, drain the pasta and add it to the sauce. Plate and serve immediately with freshly grated Parmesan to taste.

Wanderer's spaghetti

SPAGHETTI ALLA CARRETTIERA

V/Ve

serves 4

The name of this dish comes courtesy of Sicilian history. A *carrettiere*, literally, is a 'cart driver', and so this is spaghetti 'in the style of a cart driver'. This doesn't exactly roll off the tongue, so we prefer to call it 'wanderer's spaghetti', as it was created by traders who wandered the countryside of Sicily, stopping in towns to sell basic goods.

This sort of itinerant lifestyle did not lend itself to long or lavish food preparation; instead, the cart drivers relied on the same ingredients they peddled to feed themselves. *Pasta alla carrettiera* is therefore a quintessential recipe of *cucina povera*, or the poor man's kitchen, which denotes a way of cooking in southern Italy that uses affordable, unpretentious ingredients while delivering great flavour.

500g spaghetti

4 tbsp extra virgin olive oil

*1 garlic clove, peeled and
   lightly crushed*

*½ fresh red chilli, finely diced
   (optional)*

70g sun-dried tomatoes, chopped

*25g capers, washed and
   roughly chopped*

15–20g fresh parsley, finely chopped

80g toasted breadcrumbs, to serve

1. Bring a pot of generously salted water to the boil. Cook the pasta until al dente, following the packet instructions. While the pasta cooks, prepare the sauce.

2. Place the olive oil, garlic, chilli (if using) and tomatoes in a large frying pan over a medium heat. Fry for a couple of minutes, then add the capers. Remove and discard the garlic clove.

3. Once the pasta is al dente, reserve a cup of the starchy pasta cooking water, then drain the pasta and add it to the pan with the sauce. Toss to combine, adding a splash of the cooking water. Continue mixing until the sauce coats the pasta, then add the parsley and stir to combine.

4. Plate and serve immediately, topped with the toasted breadcrumbs.

Tagliatelle with prawns & lemon

TAGLIATELLE CON GAMBERONI E LIMONE   *serves 4*

If you've ever had the fortune of driving along the coastline of southern Italy, you might be familiar with the small, family-run restaurants that appear regularly on the horizon. As you get closer, you can't help but marvel at how pretty their pale blue facades look against the sun: a sort of seaside fairytale. But it's the waft of fresh seafood coming from the kitchens that is most captivating. *Gamberoni*, or prawns, are a staple on the menus here. Sourced by local fishermen in the morning and prepared the same day for lunch, often simply with garlic and lemon, they are as fresh as can be.

This recipe is inspired by our own pit stops along the Italian coastline, when, after a long drive, the promise of fresh seafood, served unpretentiously but beautifully, is too much to resist.

500g tagliatelle
1 garlic clove, minced
4 tbsp extra virgin olive oil
200g raw tiger prawns, peeled
  and deveined
25g capers, rinsed
Grated zest of ½ unwaxed lemon
Salt and black pepper, to taste

1. Bring a pot of generously salted water to the boil. Cook the pasta until al dente, following the packet instructions. While the pasta cooks, prepare the sauce.
2. In a frying pan, fry the garlic in the olive oil for around 1 minute, being careful not to burn it. Once fragrant, add the prawns, capers, salt and pepper and fry gently for 5 minutes.
3. Once the pasta is al dente, drain the pasta and add it to the pan with the sauce. Toss together and leave to cook for a minute longer. Remove from the heat and stir through the lemon zest. Plate and serve immediately.

Gnocchi with sage butter sauce

GNOCCHI AL BURRO E SALVIA

serves 4

When we visit the northern reaches of Italy, especially the picturesque Alpine villages of Lombardy, nothing brings us greater rapture than freshly made gnocchi with sage butter. As its name suggests, *burro e salvia* ('butter and sage') is the product of just two simple ingredients: butter and fresh sage leaves, fried together in a pan.

If you aren't a gnocchi enthusiast, you can pair this sauce with just about any pasta shape for a simple meal. It's also a ubiquitous pairing for filled pasta: tortellini, ravioli and other filled shapes are often anointed with *burro e salvia* before being served. You could also substitute other herbs to create different takes on this sauce – fresh rosemary or thyme, for example, are great alternatives.

500g gnocchi
150g unsalted butter
15 fresh sage leaves, finely sliced
Salt and black pepper, to taste
Parmesan, or vegetarian alternative,
*   to serve*

1. Cook the gnocchi, following the packet instructions. While the gnocchi cook, prepare the sauce.
2. Melt the butter in a large frying pan and add the sage leaves. Fry for 3–4 minutes until the sage is crisp and the butter takes on a hazelnut-brown colour. Add salt and pepper to taste.
3. Add the cooked gnocchi to the sage butter, tossing the mixture until the dumplings are completely coated.
4. Plate and serve immediately with freshly grated Parmesan to taste.

THE POETRY OF PASTA

LONG AGO IN THE KINGDOM OF ITALY, where the royal court still held sway, there lived a princess named Mafalda. A gentle girl with long, brown ringlets and a love of music, Mafalda was born in 1902 to the House of Savoy. Her upbringing, in a villa on the outskirts of Rome, was unusually modest for a princess: her mother, Queen Elena, wished for her daughter to lead a simple life, but it was also full of love. It is said that her doting mother, concerned by her daughter's delicate constitution, weighed her daily to ensure she gained weight. Mafalda, concerned in equal measure for the worrying Queen, concealed an ever-increasing number of coins in her clothing to allay her mother's fears. Until one day a handful of coins fell out and Queen Elena's worrying resumed. However, nothing in Princess Mafalda's childhood portended the tragedy of her later life.

Queen Elena would outlive Mafalda by nearly a decade, but not because of the girl's frailty. On the contrary, Mafalda is remembered by the Italian people as a lioness, having spoken out in defence of the Jews and fallen foul of Adolf Hitler. In the Second World War, Princess Mafalda of Savoy was arrested by the Gestapo and transported to Buchenwald concentration camp, where she died in 1944.

It took over 50 years for the Italian government to honour Mafalda, finally releasing a commemorative postage stamp in 1995. The Italian people, meanwhile, had taken matters into their own hands, creating for their lioness the greatest possible honour: a pasta shape in her memory. Long, wavy and with ribbon-shaped edges, mafaldine (or reginette, 'little queens') evoke Mafalda's ringlets. In this way, she lives on until such time as Italians cease to enjoy pasta.

In the realm of pasta poetry, though, Mafalda's elegy is unique. Pasta shapes (and especially their names) more often conjure up delicious in-jokes. Strozzapreti ('priest-chokers') is a hand-rolled shape popular in Emilia-Romagna, and nonne across Italy speculate on the origins of the shape's name. Some say it was a commentary on fat cat priests, choking as they gorged themselves on pasta. Others insist dutiful wives made this wholly satisfying pasta for the local priest in lieu of rent, while their husbands looked on, secretly willing the priest to choke on his meal. Strangulaprievete ('priest strangler'), a type of gnocchi found to the south, in Campania, indicates that this sentiment was not just the preserve of jealous husbands in Emilia-Romagna.

Whatever the shape, one thing is clear to us: as far as pasta names go, Italians have no appetite for the mundane. Even the more literal varieties have a poetic ring. Campanelle are 'little bells', tubes of pasta flaring out at one end like church bells. Farfalle, beloved by children throughout Italy, are 'butterflies', crimped in the middle to give each farfalla two delicate wings. Linguine are 'little tongues', while Roberta's beloved orecchiette are 'little ears'. Even the everyday fusilli are said to be derived from *fusile*, or 'rifles'; in your mind's eye, you can almost see each tight corkscrew shooting forth from the barrel.

Linguine are 'little tongues', while Roberta's beloved orecchiette are 'little ears'

Each year, the town of Castelfranco Emilia, in the province of Modena, celebrates its role in pasta folklore, for legend has it that the tortellini shape was conceived here. The story goes that Venus, Goddess of love, once spent the night there to rest her weary soul. The innkeeper, spying through a keyhole, was overcome, rushing to his kitchen to prepare fresh pasta inspired by 'the sight of the divine navel'. Tortellini, the creation of the voyeur innkeeper, have stood the test of time, and are sometimes referred to as *ombelico*, or 'belly button'. Poetry in form *and* word.

Through this propensity to create poetry from pasta, we are reminded of Italians' uniquely playful spirit. Most of all, we are reminded of the very real significance of pasta in their daily lives. Pasta is a vessel through which Italians crack jokes, tell stories, document their history and invoke legend. Whether eulogising the tragic Princess Mafalda or paying homage to the working girls of Naples (*pasta alla puttanesca*), we relish Italy's anthology of pasta poetry. With most sources recognising around 350 pasta shapes, and many more undiscovered in small towns, villages and kitchens across Italy, our quest to uncover new pasta poetry is likely to go on for some time.

Malloreddus with broad bean pesto

MALLOREDDUS AL PESTO DI FAVE

serves 4

Broad beans, also known as fava beans, are surely one of nature's greatest gifts. They are oversized when compared with the garden pea, and, in our opinion, infinitely more interesting. When broad beans come into season in spring, few things bring us greater joy than popping them out of their pretty pods.

In the region of Liguria, where pesto was born, they also play a supporting role to the better-known *pesto alla genovese*. Cherished by the townspeople of Sestri Levante, some fifty kilometres along the Italian Riviera from the regional capital of Genoa, fava beans are the key ingredient of their very own pesto. Ostensibly, the people of Sestri Levante have innovated a different, yet equally green, pesto to spite their neighbours in the capital. Truth be told, though, it's just as good, albeit in an altogether different way. To us, it's clear the people of Sestri Levante wanted not to outdo their fellow Ligurians, but provide a different perspective on pesto. It's one we are happy to embrace.

35g pine nuts
800g broad beans, parboiled for
  2–3 minutes
100ml extra virgin olive oil
100g pecorino Romano, or
  vegetarian alternative,
  grated, plus extra to serve
10 fresh mint leaves, finely chopped
1 garlic clove, minced
750g malloreddus

1. Gently toast the pine nuts in a dry frying pan over a medium-high heat until fragrant, around 2–3 minutes. Keep the kernels moving to prevent them burning.
2. Place the broad beans in a blender with the olive oil, pecorino Romano, toasted pine nuts, mint and garlic and blend until the mixture is creamy.
3. Bring a pot of generously salted water to the boil. Cook the pasta until al dente, following the packet instructions.
4. Once the pasta is al dente, drain and return to the pot, then add the pesto and toss to combine.
5. Plate and serve immediately with freshly grated pecorino Romano.

Roman cheese & pepper spaghetti

SPAGHETTI CACIO E PEPE

serves 4

Cacio e pepe, literally 'cheese and pepper', is perhaps the most recognisable dish of modern Roman cuisine. Take an evening stroll through the back streets of the Eternal City and watch as Romans, dining at their favourite *trattorie*, skilfully twist tangles of luminous cheesy spaghetti around their forks.

This is one of those sauces that feels both basic and decadent, the climax of just three ingredients: freshly ground black pepper, an almost unseemly volume of pecorino Romano, and, of course, pasta. The trick we employ here – using a little of the starchy water the pasta cooks in to thicken the sauce – is common in Italy. At first, it might feel odd to add water to thicken a sauce, but as the water evaporates, the remaining starches help the underlying ingredients to adhere (in this case, the *cacio* with the *pepe*). Pasta science, courtesy of the Roman kitchen!

500g spaghetti
1–2 tsp black peppercorns
280g pecorino Romano,
*   or vegetarian alternative,*
*   grated*

1. Bring a pot of generously salted water to the boil. Cook the pasta until al dente, following the packet instructions. While the pasta cooks, prepare the sauce.
2. With a pestle and mortar, lightly crush the black peppercorns.
3. In a bowl, mix the pecorino Romano with a splash of the starchy pasta cooking water until creamy.
4. Add the peppercorns to a pan over a low heat and gently toast for a minute. Then, add a ladleful of the starchy pasta cooking water.
5. Once the pasta is al dente, reserve another cup of the cooking water, then drain the pasta and add it to the pan containing the pepper. Turn off the heat, add the cheese mixture and toss until well combined. If necessary, add more cooking water until you obtain a creamy consistency.
6. Plate and serve immediately.

Orecchiette with Romanesco

ORECCHIETTE CON ROMANESCO

serves 4

The Romanesco broccoli is one of nature's most beautiful gifts. As though its pale, pastel-like green ('chartreuse', officially) wasn't interesting enough, scientists have identified greater virtue still in its 'fractal-esque' nature. The heads that make up the Romanesco broccoli are near identical; all that differs is their size. We just think they look a bit like alien Christmas trees.

In any case, this special variety has been harvested on the Italian peninsula since the seventeenth century and is now eaten across Italy. More akin in flavour to cauliflower than broccoli, Romanesco can be distinguished by its gentle, nutty character. We love it served simply, when its unique flavour and interesting shape take centre stage, as in this recipe.

600g Romanesco broccoli,
*   broken down into florets*
500g orecchiette
1 garlic clove, peeled and
*   lightly crushed*
1 whole fresh red chilli, cut in half
5 tbsp extra virgin olive oil
Salt and black pepper, to taste
2 tbsp grated pecorino Romano,
*   or vegetarian alternative,*
*   to serve*
Handful of fresh parsley, finely
*   chopped, to serve (optional)*

1. Bring a pot of generously salted water to the boil. Cook the Romanesco florets for 5 minutes, then strain using a slotted spoon and set aside, keeping the water boiling to cook the pasta.
2. Cook the pasta until al dente, following the packet instructions. While the pasta cooks, finish preparing the Romanesco.
3. Fry the garlic and chilli halves in the olive oil for a couple of minutes before adding the Romanesco florets and frying for a further minute or so. Remove and discard the garlic and chilli.
4. Once the pasta is al dente, drain and add to the pan with the sauce, tossing to combine.
5. Serve immediately, topped with the freshly grated pecorino Romano and parsley, if using.

Gnocchi with Parmesan cream

GNOCCHI CON CREMA AL PARMIGIANO

serves 4

A while ago we visited Parma, in the region of Emilia-Romagna, famous for its eponymous *prosciutto di Parma*. Of course, as the name hints, Parma is also renowned for its production of Parmigiano-Reggiano cheese. While dining at Ristorante Cocchi, the proprietor explained to us that this special and internationally exported *formaggio* is protected under European law, and so, legally, can only be produced in Parma, as well as a handful of adjacent provinces. This is why you might encounter the far less glamorous-sounding but similar-tasting 'Italian hard cheese' and wonder what the difference is – usually, only where it has been produced!

This sauce is our celebration of the 'King of Cheeses'. We recommend experimenting with cheeses of different ages to find the variety that delights you the most. Our favourite is Vacche Rosse, produced from the milk of rare breed red cows from the region and aged for around 24 months.

500g gnocchi

250ml whole milk

35g unsalted butter

30g plain white flour

230g Parmesan, or vegetarian alternative, grated, plus extra to serve

Salt, to taste

1. Cook the gnocchi, following the packet instructions. While the gnocchi cook, prepare the sauce.
2. In a saucepan, gently heat the milk.
3. Meanwhile, in a second saucepan, melt the butter. When the butter has completely melted, add the flour and whisk vigorously.
4. Add the hot milk, a little at a time, whisking continuously. Once all the milk has been added, leave the sauce to thicken slightly, whisking all the time. You can choose the consistency you prefer, but Roberta recommends keeping the sauce a little runny.
5. When the sauce has reached the desired consistency, add the grated Parmesan and a pinch of salt and mix well.
6. Add the cooked gnocchi to the sauce, tossing the mixture until the dumplings are completely coated.
7. Plate and serve immediately, topped with freshly grated Parmesan to taste.

Spaghetti with courgette carbonara

SPAGHETTI ALLA CARBONARA DI ZUCCHINE

As the classic carbonara recipe (see page 27) calls for guanciale (a cured cut from a pig's cheek), it is unsuitable for vegetarians. For those who have taken up vegetarianism later in life – and Finn did for several years – the passing of carbonara from one's life can cause untold gastronomic grief. Fortunately, this green version promises to restore the joy of even the most maudlin new vegetarian.

It must be said, too, that Finn was strongly opposed to Roberta's idea of *pasta alla carbonara* made with courgettes. Although he loves the mild, fresh flavour of courgettes, their very mildness seemed to make them a futile substitute for guanciale. Today, though, he is a convert. As courgettes have a fantastic ability to absorb salt, they can, if fried punctiliously and not to the point of mushiness, emulate salty morsels of guanciale while bringing a light freshness in their own right.

500g spaghetti
2 tbsp extra virgin olive oil
1 garlic clove, peeled and
  lightly crushed
2 large courgettes (around 300g),
  roughly diced
5 medium egg yolks
50g pecorino Romano, or
  vegetarian alternative, grated
15g fresh parsley, finely chopped
Salt and black pepper, to taste

1. Bring a pot of generously salted water to the boil. Cook the pasta until al dente, following the packet instructions. While the pasta cooks, prepare the sauce.
2. Heat the oil in a pan over a medium heat. Add the garlic and sauté for 2 minutes until fragrant, then remove from the pan and discard. Add the courgettes to the pan, season with salt and pepper and cook for about 5 minutes, stirring occasionally.
3. Meanwhile, place the egg yolks in a bowl and whisk gently. Add the pecorino Romano and a dash of salt and pepper and continue whisking until smooth.
4. Once the pasta is al dente, reserve a cup of the starchy pasta cooking water, then drain the pasta and add it to the pan with the courgettes. Stir to combine and cook for 1 minute over a high heat. Add the parsley then turn off the heat.
5. Slowly add the egg mixture, stirring quickly with a wooden spoon to distribute throughout the pasta. If the mixture becomes dry, add a splash of the cooking water and toss vigorously to combine.
6. Plate and serve immediately, topped with freshly ground black pepper to taste.

Orecchiette pasta salad with tomato & ricotta

ORECCHIETTE ALLA CRUDAIOLA

serves 4

In Puglia, it's common for temperatures to exceed 40°C in the summer. On these days, Roberta and the other women living on the d'Elia farm are loath to labour in the kitchen for long, yet the family's inclination to eat pasta is no less pronounced because of the heat. Instead, pasta simply adapts. This recipe takes minutes to prepare, minimising time spent in hot kitchens where air conditioning is more the exception than the rule. *Pasta alla crudaiola* is also refreshing, served cold to provide lunchtime respite from the unrelenting heat.

500g orecchiette

350g fresh cherry tomatoes, chopped

10g fresh basil leaves, finely chopped, plus extra to serve

6–7 tbsp extra virgin olive oil, plus extra to serve

½ garlic clove, peeled and minced

30g ricotta salata, coarsely grated, plus extra to serve

Salt, to taste

1. Bring a pot of generously salted water to the boil. Cook the pasta until al dente, following the packet instructions. While the pasta cooks, prepare the sauce.
2. Put the tomatoes, basil, olive oil and garlic in a bowl and stir to combine. Add the ricotta salata and stir gently, then add salt to taste.
3. Once the pasta is al dente, drain and rinse under the cold tap water to cool the pasta. Toss the pasta with the tomato mixture.
4. Serve with a drizzle of extra virgin olive oil on top, along with a few leaves of fresh basil and some freshly grated ricotta salata.

Four cheese gnocchi

GNOCCHI AL QUATTRO FORMAGGI   *serves 4*

As the name suggests, this is one for the cheese lovers. If you aren't one of them, look away now. Shamelessly indulgent, this recipe brings together four fantastic cheeses of Italy, namely *mozzarella di bufala*, fontina, Parmigiano-Reggiano and Gorgonzola.

If the mention of Gorgonzola, a blue cheese, does not inspire enthusiasm on your part, do not worry. When combined with its fellow *formaggi*, the pungency of the Gorgonzola is severely curtailed, leaving behind a wonderful saltiness. This is real cucina di casa: food perfect for a cold winter's night. A good glass of red makes it even more comforting.

100g Gorgonzola
100g mozzarella
100g fontina or Gruyère
100g Parmesan
125ml double cream
500g gnocchi
Salt and black pepper, to taste

1. Cut the cheeses into small pieces and set aside.
2. Gently heat the double cream in a saucepan and add the pieces of cheese. Cook over a low heat for 5 minutes, stirring all the time, to help the cheeses melt into the cream.
3. Meanwhile, cook the gnocchi, following the packet instructions, then transfer the cooked gnocchi a few at a time to the saucepan with the cheese sauce. Stir to combine.
4. Serve immediately with freshly ground black pepper to taste.

Make your own
TOMATO SAUCE

Sometimes, we don't have time to find a recipe, check that we have all the ingredients and go to the shops to get those things we're missing. Sometimes, we don't have the energy to try a new dish, and more often than not there are leftover ingredients in the freezer that need to be used up. These 'Make Your Own' pages are designed to help you in these moments. From the most basic tomato sauce, you can create three delicious meals, inspired by three of Italy's regions.

BASE RECIPE (SERVES 4)

- Choose your preferred additions from the regions opposite.
- Gently fry 1 garlic clove, peeled and lightly crushed, in 2 tbsp olive oil for a couple of minutes until fragrant, then discard the garlic.
- Add 400g chopped tinned or fresh tomatoes to the garlic-infused oil.
- Add 1 tsp sea salt flakes and 15g fresh basil leaves.
- Cover and cook gently for up to 30 minutes. Add a splash of water from time to time if the sauce becomes too thick.

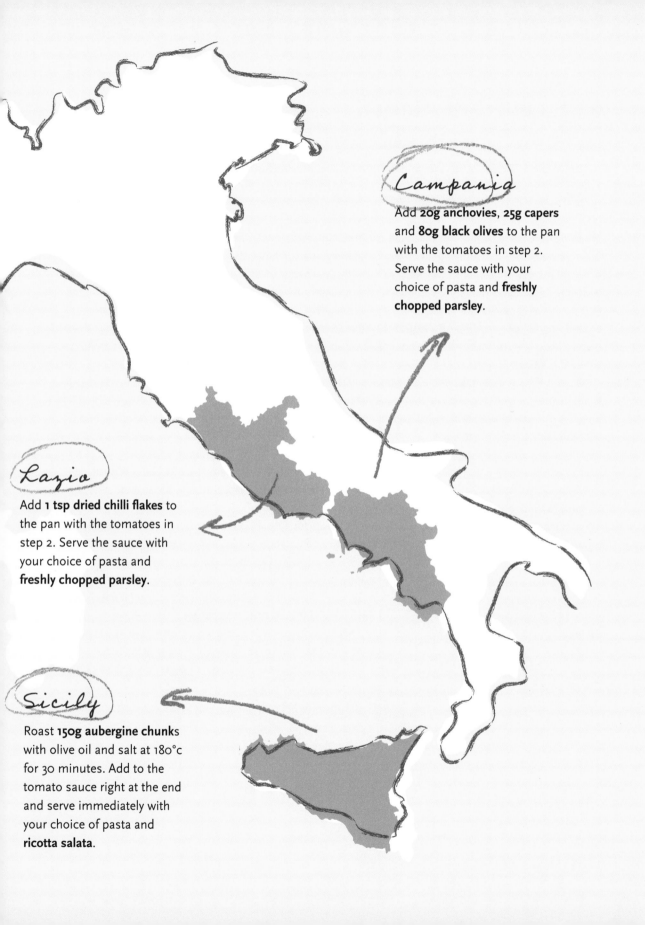

Campania

Add **20g anchovies**, **25g capers** and **80g black olives** to the pan with the tomatoes in step 2. Serve the sauce with your choice of pasta and **freshly chopped parsley**.

Lazio

Add **1 tsp dried chilli flakes** to the pan with the tomatoes in step 2. Serve the sauce with your choice of pasta and **freshly chopped parsley**.

Sicily

Roast **150g aubergine chunk**s with olive oil and salt at 180°c for 30 minutes. Add to the tomato sauce right at the end and serve immediately with your choice of pasta and **ricotta salata**.

Spaghetti with clams

SPAGHETTI ALLE VONGOLE

serves 4

When we were talking about this dish with our friend Imma, who is from the region of Campania where it originates, she told us a story about an iconic Neapolitan actor, Eduardo De Filippo. Apparently, at the end of one of his shows in 1947, he was so tired that he could barely muster the strength to visit the restaurant with his co-stars (and siblings) Peppino and Titina. As he got home, however, hunger struck and a pantry raid yielded a scant variety of ingredients: merely spaghetti, parsley, garlic, chilli and cherry tomatoes. Eduardo persevered, rustling up a dish that he dubbed *spaghetti alle vongole fujate*. In the local Neapolitan dialect, *fujate* means 'escaped', so in Eduardo's version of *spaghetti alle vongole* ('spaghetti with clams'), you won't find a single clam.

In the following days, the people of Naples sought to emulate their beloved actor, eschewing clams as never before, much to the chagrin of the city's seafood vendors. Luckily for them, though, the fad didn't last long, and Neapolitans quickly reignited their love affair with the real *spaghetti alle vongole*, which lives on with the same passion to this day.

500g spaghetti

1kg clams, soaked in plenty of water for 1 hour

8 tbsp extra virgin olive oil

2 garlic cloves, peeled and lightly crushed

1 fresh red chilli, seeds removed and finely chopped

Salt and black pepper, to taste

Handful of fresh parsley, finely chopped, to serve

1. Bring a pot of generously salted water to the boil. Cook the pasta until al dente, following the packet instructions. While the pasta cooks, prepare the sauce.

2. Rinse the clams for a final time under fresh water and set aside.

3. Heat the olive oil in a frying pan over a medium heat with the garlic cloves and chilli. Gently fry the mixture for 3–4 minutes, then add the clams, increase the heat and cook for a few minutes, stirring every now and then until the clams have opened. Turn off the heat and discard the garlic cloves.

4. Once the pasta is al dente, reserve a cup of the starchy pasta cooking water, then drain the pasta and add it to the pan containing the clams. Add a little of the pasta cooking water and season with salt and pepper.

5. Plate and serve immediately, topped with fresh parsley.

Tagliatelle with Parma ham & cream

TAGLIATELLE PANNA E PROSCIUTTO DI PARMA *serves 4*

As a young boy growing up in Newcastle, one of Finn's formative pasta memories came courtesy of a lady called Margaret, the grandmother of his friend Matthew. On early Saturday afternoons in winter, taking a short break from playing football in the street, Finn and Matthew would visit Margaret for her pasta with bacon and cream. It was simple but delicious, providing ample energy as they returned to play in the snow until sunset.

Some two decades later, as they worked late into a winter's evening at her cottage in Biggleswade, Roberta rustled up a bowl of creamy pasta for Finn, this time with big wodges of salty *prosciutto di Parma* from her pantry. As pasta has a special way of doing, he was instantly transported back to Margaret's house in Newcastle.

500g tagliatelle
2 tbsp extra virgin olive oil
½ brown or white onion, or
* 1 shallot, finely chopped*
5 slices prosciutto cotto,
* cut into strips*
100ml single cream
Salt and black pepper, to taste
Parmesan, to serve

1. Bring a pot of generously salted water to the boil. Cook the pasta until al dente, following the packet instructions. While the pasta cooks, prepare the sauce.
2. Heat the olive oil in a large frying pan and cook the onion or shallot for around 4 minutes until golden brown in colour.
3. Add the prosciutto cotto and fry for a few minutes, then slowly pour in the cream and stir to combine. Simmer gently over a low heat, ensuring the mixture doesn't thicken too much. Add salt and pepper to taste.
4. Once the pasta is al dente, reserve a cup of the starchy pasta cooking water, then drain the pasta and add it to the pan with the sauce. Toss to combine over a medium heat. If the pasta gets too dry, add half of the reserved cooking water and stir gently to combine.
5. Plate and serve immediately, topped with freshly ground black pepper and freshly grated Parmesan to taste.

Spaghetti with olive oil, garlic & chilli

SPAGHETTI AGLIO, OLIO E PEPERONCINO

V/Ve

serves 4

Finn first encountered this staple pasta dish as a European exchange student in Vienna. He was living with an Italian girl, Chiara, from Naples. In their student halls, it was customary for each student to prepare a typical dinner from their home country: a gastronomic take on the Eurovision Song Contest, you might say. Chiara served this sauce with bucatini, a shape similar to spaghetti but punctuated with a *buco*, or 'hole', in the centre of each strand. While the pasta shape was new to him at the time, Finn was more surprised by how the three ingredients Chiara threw together, in mere moments, yielded such a satisfying meal, one that he spent the remainder of his time in Vienna trying to emulate.

500g spaghetti

8 tbsp extra virgin olive oil

5 garlic cloves, peeled and roughly chopped

2 fresh red chillies, finely sliced (remove the seeds first for a milder flavour)

Salt, to taste

10g fresh parsley or basil leaves, finely chopped, to serve (optional)

1. Bring a pot of generously salted water to the boil. Cook the pasta until al dente, following the packet instructions. While the pasta cooks, prepare the sauce.
2. Pour the oil into a large frying pan and place over a medium heat. Add the garlic and a touch of salt. Gently sauté the garlic for 2 minutes until fragrant, being careful not to burn the mixture, then remove the pan from the heat and add the sliced chillies.
3. Once the pasta is al dente, reserve a cup of the starchy pasta cooking water, then drain the pasta and add it to the pan with the oil, garlic and chilli, along with a splash of the cooking water. Stir vigorously until the pasta is completely coated.
4. Plate and serve immediately, topped with parsley or basil, if using.

Orecchiette with rocket pesto

ORECCHIETTE AL PESTO DI RUCOLA   *serves 4*

Roberta's nonna, Maria-Assunta, largely preferred to put the wild rocket collected on their farmland to use in the classic peasant dish Orecchiette with Rocket and Potatoes (see page 176). But every once in a while (and usually at the supplication of her granddaughter), she would create a pesto from the rucola they foraged, fabulously green and full of heady flavour. To ensure the dish was equally amenable to adults, Maria-Assunta liked to add anchovies, a tradition Roberta continues to this day. While their presence might sound strange or misplaced in a pesto, we encourage you to give it a go. Far from making the pesto fishy, the anchovies just give it a salty character (and remind Roberta of her childhood). We promise you won't even know they're there.

500g orecchiette
40g blanched almonds
200g rocket, washed
4 anchovies, rinsed and
  roughly chopped
4 tbsp pecorino Romano, grated
2 tbsp Parmesan, grated,
  plus extra to serve
6–8 tbsp extra virgin olive oil
Salt and black pepper, to taste

1. Bring a pot of generously salted water to the boil. Cook the pasta until al dente, following the packet instructions. While the pasta cooks, prepare the sauce.
2. Crush the almonds using a pestle and mortar until they form a paste. Remove from the mortar and set aside.
3. Clean the pestle and mortar, then use them to grind the rocket. Once the rocket is broken down, add the anchovies and a little salt and pepper and grind to combine. Finally, return the ground almonds to the mortar and blend to combine.
4. Add the cheeses and enough extra virgin olive oil to create a creamy and rustic consistency.
5. Once the pasta is al dente, drain and add it to a bowl with the pesto. Toss to combine.
6. Plate and serve immediately with freshly grated Parmesan to taste.

Tips & Substitutions

- You could use a food processor in place of the pestle and mortar in this recipe. Pulse the ingredients roughly to preserve a rustic consistency.

PART 2

20 MINUTES

Imagine a languorous late afternoon in the far southern region of Calabria. You take an outdoor seat at a café, legs in the sun, your head shaded by a large awning. Settling in for the remainder of the day, you watch the world pass by. Nuns lick brightly coloured gelato from cones, dogs lie on the hot cobblestones, and Mount Stromboli, an active volcano straddling an eponymous island in the Tyrrhenian Sea, can be seen on the horizon.

As the sun lowers and the warm Calabrian evening sets in, you wander a short distance to a family-owned trattoria. It's rumoured the place is run by a local 'Ndrangheta (Calabrian Mafia) family, but you wouldn't know and don't really mind anyway: the donna, Elisabetta, is soft-spoken with a gentle smile and shows you to your table. You pick over an antipasti of *capicollo* (a type of charcuterie enjoyed in the region) and whet your appetite with a small glass of Gaglioppo wine from the local vineyard. The pace is unhurried and there is no rush to order. Elisabetta places a pastel bowl of olives on your table as she steps outside for a cigarette.

You spend some time watching other people's chosen dishes go by: platters of blushing pink prawns, salt-baked sea bass deboned tableside, and bowls of tiny octopus morsels small enough to pop in your mouth. Elisabetta's home-made pasta looks irresistible, though: ribbons of tagliatelle, coated in a coral-coloured sauce of mascarpone cheese, lemon and Calabria's chilli-laced 'nduja, a sort of spicy sausage paste. Another diner is devouring a bright green bowl of pistachio pesto, which is actually a speciality of nearby Sicily, but no less loved here. The tang of Parmigiano-Reggiano, freshly grated over diners' pasta with great generosity, is heady in the warm evening breeze.

Happily, not everything needs to be left to the imagination. In the time it would have taken you to settle into your table, order a drink and peruse the menu of this Calabrian trattoria (about 20 minutes, from experience), you could have created any of this section's gratifying pasta recipes at home.

Working girl's spaghetti

SPAGHETTI ALLA PUTTANESCA

Born in Naples, the largest city of the Campania region, puttanesca is a gutsy, tomato-based sauce, made with plenty of garlic. Traditionally, it's also made with anchovies fished in the Bay of Naples, giving it a deep, savoury taste. If you don't like anchovies, or are preparing a plant-based *puttanesca*, these can simply be left out: the fresh olives and capers provide ample salty character.

The backstory of *pasta alla puttanesca* is equally full of character. The term quite literally refers to pasta made 'in the manner of a prostitute'. *Che scandalo!* Food writers have debated its nomenclature ever since the dish emerged after the Second World War, but the common understanding is that the dish was born in Naples' *case di appuntamenti* ('appointment houses'). We hope you'll be able to infer the meaning of an *appuntamento* so we needn't utter it. As preparing the sauce was a labour of mere minutes – indeed, simply 'throwing whatever together' – this could be done between other, er, obligations.

1 garlic clove, peeled and lightly crushed

1 fresh red chilli, seeds removed and finely chopped

6 tbsp extra virgin olive oil

100g anchovies, rinsed

400g fresh tomatoes, peeled and diced

100g Gaeta (or Kalamata) olives

40g capers, rinsed

1 tsp tomato purée

500g spaghetti

Salt, to taste

Handful of fresh parsley, chopped, to serve (optional)

1. In a large frying pan over a medium heat, fry the garlic and red chilli in the oil for 2 minutes until fragrant. Once the garlic is golden brown, remove it from the pan and discard.
2. Add the anchovies to the pan and break these into smaller pieces by gently mashing them with a fork. After a minute or so, add the tomatoes, olives, capers and tomato purée and mix well. Add salt to taste and allow to cook for 10 minutes.
3. Bring a pot of generously salted water to the boil. Cook the pasta until al dente, following the packet instructions.
4. Once the pasta is al dente, reserve a cup of the starchy pasta cooking water, then drain the pasta and add it to the sauce. Toss to coat, adding a splash of the cooking water to loosen, if needed.
5. Plate and serve immediately, topped with the parsley, if using.

Orecchiette with pistachio pesto

serves 4

ORECCHIETTE AL PESTO DI PISTACCHIO

The pistachio tree (from the Greek *pistàkion*) is native to the Mediterranean basin. Its pastel green nuts are often flecked prettily with shades of pink, and are used widely across the region, from Turkey to Italy and beyond. The pistachio was prized in the Middle East by the ancient Jews, but it was the Arabs, seizing Sicily from the Byzantines in the ninth century, who first cultivated pistachio trees in the rich volcanic soils around Mount Etna, where they continue to flourish today.

In our opinion, the finest pistachios are from Bronte, a town just 16 kilometres from Mount Etna. There, they're known as the 'green gold', in reference to their importance to the local economy. And with such a munificent pistachio crop on the island, this vibrant pesto has become an undeniable classic of the Sicilian kitchen.

200g raw, unsalted pistachio nuts, shelled

15–20g fresh basil leaves, roughly torn

80g Parmesan, or vegetarian alternative, grated, plus extra to serve

1 garlic clove, halved

150ml extra virgin olive oil

500g orecchiette

Salt, to taste

1. Toast the pistachio nuts in a dry frying pan over a medium-high heat for around 3–4 minutes. Keep them moving to prevent them burning, and once lightly browned take the pan off the heat.
2. Place the basil leaves, Parmesan, garlic and a drizzle of olive oil into a mortar and grind with a pestle until creamy.
3. Add the pistachios and grind until they break down and combine with the mixture. You should have a creamy yet slightly chunky consistency. Drizzle in the remaining olive oil and continue to grind until you have a creamy paste. Add salt to taste.
4. Bring a pot of generously salted water to the boil. Cook the pasta until al dente, following the packet instructions.
5. Once the pasta is al dente, reserve a ladleful of the starchy pasta cooking water. Add this to the pesto and stir through to loosen the sauce. Drain the pasta and return it to the pan. Add the pesto and toss until the pasta is completely coated.
6. Plate and serve immediately with freshly grated Parmesan to taste.

Tips & Substitutions

- You could use a food processor in place of the pestle and mortar in this recipe. Pulse the ingredients roughly to preserve a rustic consistency.

Gnocchi from Sorrento

GNOCCHI ALLA SORRENTINA

serves 4

Naples, in the sun-drenched region of Campania, is renowned in the gastronomic world. Less renowned, but no less important in the culinary story of Campania, are the many small towns and villages dotted along the region's iconic Amalfi Coast. Sorrento, for example, perched on cliffs overlooking the Bay of Naples, gives its name to this dish.

This wholesome recipe dates back to the sixteenth century, when the first potatoes from the New World were unloaded in the town's irresistibly pretty marinas. Locals combined them with flour and eggs to form rustic dumplings. When we devour this, we like to pretend we're dining on one of Sorrento's many balconies, overlooking the coast, with the fragrance of orange blossoms heady in the air.

4 tbsp extra virgin olive oil
1 garlic clove, peeled
400g tomato passata
10g fresh basil leaves
1 tsp sea salt flakes
500g gnocchi
170g fior di latte (or buffalo)
*   mozzarella, cut into small pieces*
30g Parmesan, or vegetarian
*   alternative, grated, plus extra*
*   to serve*

1. Preheat the oven to 180°C.
2. Place the olive oil in a frying pan over a medium heat. Add the garlic and cook for 1–2 minutes until fragrant, then remove the clove from the pan and discard.
3. Add the tomato passata, half the fresh basil leaves and the salt to the pan. Turn up the heat slightly and simmer for 7–8 minutes.
4. While the sauce simmers, cook the gnocchi, following packet instructions, then transfer the cooked gnocchi to the sauce, tossing gently to coat.
5. Transfer some of the gnocchi to a 20cm baking tray to create a first layer at the bottom of the tray. Add a scattering of the mozzarella, Parmesan and basil before adding a second layer of the gnocchi. Continue this process until all of the gnocchi are in the baking tray. Top the final layer with mozzarella and Parmesan.
6. Place the baking tray in the oven for around 10 minutes until the cheese has melted.
7. Plate and serve immediately with freshly grated Parmesan to taste.

Pasta with peas

PASTA E PISELLI   *serves 2*

If two ingredients were ever to be described as a match made in heaven, they would surely be peas and pancetta. The saltiness of pancetta complements the sweetness of the humble pea so well, and this simple recipe of the Neapolitan kitchen is testament to the power of this poor man's pairing. Indeed, *pasta e piselli* was born of necessity: Naples, like much of the Italian south, was impoverished for centuries.

Despite a wholesale improvement in living standards, particularly since the postwar economic boom, this dish remains a favourite not just of Neapolitans but all Italians, and is the sort of food prepared by nonne, with love, for grandchildren across the nation.

1–2 tbsp extra virgin olive oil
1 brown or white onion, finely diced
70g pancetta, cubed
600g peas (fresh or frozen,
 both work well)
500g malloreddus
Salt and black pepper, to taste
Parmesan, grated, to serve

1. Place the oil in a saucepan over a low heat. Add the diced onion and sweat for around 5 minutes until soft, then add the pancetta and cook for an additional 5 minutes until the meat begins to crisp.
2. Add the peas to the pan, along with a splash of hot water. Cover the pan with a lid and allow the peas to steam.
3. Meanwhile, bring a pot of generously salted water to the boil. Cook the pasta until al dente, following the packet instructions.
4. While the pasta cooks, mash around half of the peas in the pan using a fork or potato masher to form a coarse purée. Give the ingredients one last stir and remove from the heat.
5. Once the pasta is al dente, reserve a cup of the starchy pasta cooking water, then drain the pasta and add it to the sauce. Toss to coat, adding a further splash of cooking water, if needed. Season to taste.
6. Plate and serve immediately with freshly grated Parmesan to taste.

Rigatoni with a spicy tomato sauce

RIGATONI ALL'ARRABBIATA

serves 4

Since the arrival of tomatoes from South America in the sixteenth century, Italians have formed an enduring love affair with the fruit, which they christened the *pomodoro* ('golden apple'). Today, hundreds of varieties are native to Italy, from Sicily's Pomodoro di Pachino to the Pomodoro di San Marzano, grown in the volcanic soils of Mount Vesuvius. Italians love to visit local markets in search of the best specimens, touching and smelling the fruit as they go. Often, they return to their homes with a glut of tomatoes to be used as the base of fresh sauces.

This sauce is one such example, originating in the region of Lazio. The inclusion of chilli flakes gives the sauce its name: *arrabbiata* ('angry') refers to its ferocious heat. Hanging chillies adorn the verandas of homes across the Italian south, so that, when the need for heat presents itself, *pasta all'arrabbiata* can be conjured up at short notice.

1 garlic clove, peeled and lightly crushed
6 tbsp extra virgin olive oil
600g quality tinned tomatoes, chopped
15g dried red chilli flakes
500g rigatoni
Salt, to taste
10g fresh parsley, finely chopped, to serve (optional)

1. In a frying pan over a medium heat, fry the garlic in the oil for 2 minutes until fragrant. Once the garlic is golden brown, remove it from the pan and discard.
2. Add the chopped tomatoes, chilli flakes and a little salt to the pan. Stir to combine and allow to simmer for 15–20 minutes over a low heat.
3. In the meantime, bring a pot of generously salted water to the boil. Cook the pasta until al dente, following the packet instructions.
4. Once the pasta is al dente, reserve a cup of the starchy pasta cooking water, then drain the pasta and add it to the sauce. Toss to coat, adding a splash of the cooking water to loosen the sauce, if needed.
5. Plate and serve immediately, topped with the parsley, if using.

WHO IS NONNA?

PUT SIMPLY, 'NONNA' IS THE ITALIAN WORD FOR GRANDMOTHER.
But this short word of just five letters invokes something far greater than
the sum of its parts. And just as Rome wasn't built in a day, so we have little
hope of deconstructing what 'nonna' *really* means to Italians in this short
chapter. Instead, to give you a glimpse into the spirit of this great character and
matriarch, we thought we'd tell you the real-life story of Roberta's nonna.

Maria-Assunta d'Elia lived in the town of Foggia in northern Puglia, in the centre
of a wheat-growing area sometimes referred to as the granary of Italy. Each day,
she spent hours standing at a broad table in the back garden, filling enormous
glass jars with fresh orecchiette, made by hand the way her mother had taught
her. Nothing but semola, water, a wooden board and hard work went into creating
this precious pasta native to Puglia. Maria-Assunta grazed each little piece of
dough with a flick of her mother's orecchiette knife, passed down to her and now
cherished by Roberta, to form the traditional shape, like a little veined ear.

This was a Sisyphean task, for no sooner had the jar been filled than it was
emptied again, because Maria-Assunta presided over an enormous family.
Her ten children all had spouses and had between two and five grandchildren
apiece. The entire family (including our Roberta) lived together in a two-building
complex, Residenza d'Elia, ruled by Maria-Assunta's firm but loving hand.

Each year, Nonna Assunta would oversee the d'Elia clan as they harvested olives
from the sprawling groves on the land. This labour began at dawn, so as to
afford time to complete the work before Puglia's ferocious sun would set in
later in the morning. Together, under Maria-Assunta's supervision, the family
would hand-press extra virgin olive oil from the crop, enduring the hard work
and sour smell of the olives to provide oil for the family to use throughout the
year. During this time, Maria-Assunta would arbitrate family disputes, discipline
unruly children (notably Roberta), and spin the most unlikely (and often entirely
fictional) stories. With the maiden name 'Coppola', Maria-Assunta's favourite gag

involved her insisting to her grandchildren that she was, in fact, the cousin of the famous Hollywood director.

In high summer, when temperatures soared into the 30s, she took vast piles of the fresh tomatoes that Foggia is known for and transformed them into rich, smooth passata, picking through bunches of basil leaves. Maria-Assunta pressed her granddaughters into service making orecchiette and passata, believing this to be an important preparation to be good wives and home-makers.

Like many nonne across Italy, Maria-Assunta understood the value of hard work and frugality. A teenager during the First World War, she grew up in lean times. A mother in the Second World War, she left Puglia to escape the invading forces and the bombings, making her way by foot, children in hand, across the fields to Calabria, the adjacent region to the west of Puglia. Having lived on farms all her life, she knew which herbs were edible, which were poisonous, and which needed to be cooked to rid them of prickles. As they went from town to town, she bought semola flour from the locals and made orecchiette to remind her family of home.

the family would hand-press extra virgin olive oil from the crop, enduring the hard work and sour smell of the olives to provide oil for the family to use throughout the year.

Almost half a century later, when Roberta came to know her nonna in more peaceful and prosperous times, it seemed that Maria-Assunta had always been old and wise. She had beautiful, soft skin, golden from many days spent in the sun making pasta, yet wizened by its rays and the difficulties she had endured. Maria-Assunta spent her days petting her cat, Laura, imparting words of wisdom and confidence to her grandchildren, and making pasta day in and day out.

Nonna Assunta has long passed, but Roberta still uses her knife, passed down through the generations, to make their treasured orecchiette. Stoic, comforting, repository of tradition, anchor of the family. Nonna.

Gnocchi with basil pesto

GNOCCHI AL PESTO

This dish is close to the heart of our co-founder, Alessandro, who grew up in Genoa, the city that gives its name to this pesto. As a child, his nonna, Maddalena, would prepare fresh *pesto alla Genovese* as he watched, crushing (Italian has a better verb, pestare) the fresh ingredients by hand in her stone mortar with a heavy pestle.

You can use a food processor here if you must, but we'd urge you to resist this. One of the joys of authentic pesto is its rustic texture, which comes courtesy of a good pestle and mortar workout. We've paired it with gnocchi, as this is what Alessandro's nonna served her pesto with, but any pasta shape works well. Use the freshest basil and very best extra virgin olive oil you can find: the quality of the ingredients makes all the difference when preparing pesto.

15g pine nuts

80g fresh basil leaves, roughly chopped

40g Parmesan, or vegetarian alternative, grated, plus extra to serve

25g pecorino Romano, or vegetarian alternative, grated

½ garlic clove, minced

6 tbsp extra virgin olive oil

250g gnocchi

Salt, to taste

1. Gently toast the pine nuts in a dry frying pan over a medium-high heat until fragrant, around 2–3 minutes. Keep the kernels moving to prevent them burning.

2. Place the basil, Parmesan, pecorino Romano, garlic and 2 tablespoons of the extra virgin olive oil in a mortar and grind with a pestle until creamy.

3. Add the pine nuts and grind until combined with the oil and basil mixture. You should have a creamy yet slightly chunky consistency. Drizzle in the remaining olive oil and continue to grind until you have a creamy paste.

4. Cook the gnocchi, following the packet instructions, then return the cooked gnocchi to the pan with the pesto and toss until coated.

5. Plate and serve immediately with freshly grated Parmesan to taste.

Tips & Substitutions

- You could use a food processor in place of the pestle and mortar in this recipe. Pulse the ingredients roughly to preserve a rustic consistency.

Tagliatelle with smoked salmon

TAGLIATELLE AL SALMONE AFFUMICATO

serves 2

Pasta al salmone seemed to have its heyday in the 1980s, when smoked salmon was en vogue. Although smoked salmon has since lost something of its lustre, this dish is fortunately no less delicious today.

Like so many others in the book, this recipe calls for only a few ingredients, so it is important to use the best smoked salmon you can find as it will make all the difference. We get ours from our friends at Daylesford, an organic farm in Gloucestershire. It's worth mentioning, too, that because of its egg constituent, fresh pasta is preferred here. Although preparing your own tagliatelle (see page 222) might sound onerous, we promise it isn't. More importantly, it'll elevate your *pasta al salmone* to new heights. Remember, if using fresh, you'll want 200g of pasta per person.

2 tbsp unsalted butter
½ brown or white onion, finely chopped
125g smoked salmon, roughly chopped
100ml double cream
250g tagliatelle
Black pepper, to taste

1. Melt the butter in a frying pan over a medium heat. Add the onion and cook for 4 minutes until browned, then add the salmon, cooking for around 1 minute until opaque. Slowly add the cream and cook until the sauce has thickened slightly.
2. Bring a pot of generously salted water to the boil. Cook the pasta until al dente, following the packet instructions.
3. Once the pasta is al dente, reserve a cup of the starchy pasta cooking water, then drain the pasta and add to the sauce. Toss to coat, adding a splash of the cooking water to loosen the sauce, if needed.
4. Plate and serve immediately with freshly ground black pepper to taste.

Rigatoni with radicchio & Gorgonzola

RIGATONI AL RADICCHIO E GORGONZOLA   *serves 6*

Radicchio is a type of chicory from Italy that counts Roberta among its biggest fans. It owes its remarkable colour to a Belgian agronomist, Francesco Van den Borre, who arrived in the Italian region of Veneto in the nineteenth century and used a whitening process to transform the green pigmentation of radicchio into white and deep red. Pasta with radicchio looks (and tastes) fantastic and is certain to impress guests, particularly when served with salty, blue-veined Gorgonzola cheese, as here.

3 tbsp extra virgin olive oil
1 shallot, finely diced
1 head of radicchio, cleaned
  and sliced
150g prosciutto di Parma,
  cut into strips
300g Gorgonzola
750g rigatoni
40g Parmesan, to serve
Salt and black pepper, to taste

1. Heat the oil in a frying pan and fry the shallot until golden brown. Add the radicchio and 100ml of water (around half a glass) and let it cook over a medium heat for 10 minutes.
2. In a separate pan, dry fry the prosciutto for 2–3 minutes over a medium-high heat until crisp, then add it to the radicchio.
3. If the sauce is too dry, add a drop of water. Then add the Gorgonzola and stir until completely melted. Once it reaches a creamy consistency, remove the sauce from the heat and season to taste.
4. Bring a pot of generously salted water to the boil. Cook the pasta until al dente, following the packet instructions. Once the pasta is al dente, drain and add to the sauce, tossing to coat.
5. Plate and serve immediately with freshly grated Parmesan to taste.

Venetian spaghetti

SPAGHETTI ALLA VENETA

serves 6

Like many other regions of the country, Veneto, in the northeast of Italy, has its own dialect. Known as *Veneto*, its four million or so speakers are more likely to regard it as a language than a dialect. Venetians are fiercely proud of their heritage (the Republic of Venice was once a major maritime power) and arguably favour visitors speaking the vernacular, so those planning a trip to the region would do well to know some of the lingo.

This recipe is inspired by Venice's *spaghetti alla busara*, a pasta dish with tomatoes and scampi. It's said to take its name from the Venetian word *busièra*, or 'liar', perhaps in reference to the way the tomatoes conceal the seafood within. As Roberta doesn't like to lie (or perhaps more saliently tends to prefer seafood without tomatoes), we've forgone the fruit in this recipe for full-frontal seafood flavour.

15g fresh parsley, finely chopped

3 tbsp breadcrumbs

6 tbsp extra virgin olive oil

2 garlic cloves, peeled

16 large raw king prawns, peeled, deveined and washed

150–200ml white wine

1 tsp sweet paprika

500g spaghetti

Salt and black pepper, to taste

1. Combine the parsley and breadcrumbs in a bowl.
2. Heat the olive oil in a large non-stick pan over a medium heat, add the garlic cloves and cook for 2 minutes, letting them brown slightly and become fragrant, then remove and discard the garlic.
3. Add the prawns to the pan, arranging them in a single layer, and cook for a couple of minutes before adding the white wine. Carefully flip each prawn and continue to cook. Season with the paprika and salt and remove from the heat.
4. Sprinkle the parsley and breadcrumb mixture over the contents of the pan.
5. Bring a pot of generously salted water to the boil. Cook the pasta until al dente, following the packet instructions.
6. Once the pasta is al dente, drain the pasta and add to the pan with the prawns, tossing to coat. Sauté for a couple of minutes, then plate and serve immediately, topped with ground black pepper.

Pappardelle with golden tomatoes

PAPPARDELLE CON DATTERINI FRESCHI GIALLI

V/Ve

serves 4

Tomatoes are surely one of the greatest blessings bestowed by nature on humanity. They are held up as a prime example of umami, one of the five basic tastes, which is essentially savouriness. But tomatoes can also be wonderfully sweet. Yellow and orange tomatoes in particular contain very little acid and are notably sweeter than their red-skinned siblings. We like to roast them with good olive oil and garlic, and devour them with freshly torn basil. Sunshine on a plate.

450g yellow and/or orange
*   tomatoes, halved*
8 tbsp extra virgin olive oil
1 tsp fresh oregano leaves,
*   removed from stem*
500g pappardelle
15–20g fresh basil leaves,
*   roughly torn*
Salt and pepper, to taste
Chilli oil, to serve (optional)

1. Preheat the oven to 200°C and line a baking tray with parchment paper.
2. Place the tomatoes on the tray, drizzle with the olive oil and season with salt and oregano. Roast the tomatoes for 5 minutes, then reduce the oven temperature to 180°C and roast for a further 5 minutes, ensuring the tomatoes don't blister or char too much. Once cooked, remove from the oven and set aside to cool slightly.
3. In the meantime, bring a pot of generously salted water to the boil. Cook the pasta until al dente, following the packet instructions.
4. Once the pasta is al dente, drain the pasta and return to the pot with the roasted tomatoes, stirring to combine and breaking down the tomatoes slightly as you mix. Add the shredded basil and salt to taste (you may require more than you think to offset the sweetness of the tomatoes).
5. Plate and serve immediately, topped with a drizzle of chilli oil, if desired.

Tagliatelle with courgette, mint & chilli

TAGLIATELLE CON PESTO DI ZUCCHINE,
MENTA E PEPERONCINO

V/Ve

serves 4

Courgettes are relative newcomers to Italian cuisine, having first been cultivated in Italy only in the nineteenth century. Since then, production has proliferated owing to the fruit's agreeable flavour and the squash's willingness to grow. Unfortunately, as with many other gifts from the botanical world (notably tomatoes), we have come to expect courgettes year-round, even when they are far from their best.

We heartily recommend you prepare this dish during the summer months, when courgettes are in season and full of bright, fresh flavour. If you can, visit a farmers' market and pick out a kaleidoscope of different colours and shapes. While supermarket shelves would suggest otherwise, courgettes come in a multitude of varieties and will fill your kitchen with sunshine.

2 tbsp extra virgin olive oil
4 courgettes, washed and diced
½ garlic clove, minced
½ fresh red chilli, seeds removed and finely chopped
10–15g fresh mint leaves, finely chopped
50g Parmesan, or vegetarian alternative, grated, plus extra to serve
50g blanched almonds
500g tagliatelle
Salt and black pepper, to taste

1. Heat the olive oil in a large frying pan over a medium heat. Add the courgettes, garlic and chilli along with a splash of water and fry gently for around 10 minutes until the courgettes start to soften. Season with salt and pepper to taste.
2. Once the courgettes are cooked, remove the pan from the heat and allow the mixture to cool before transferring to a food processor. Add the mint, Parmesan and almonds and pulse until a creamy yet rustic sauce is formed.
3. Bring a pot of generously salted water to the boil. Cook the pasta until al dente, following the packet instructions.
4. Once the pasta is al dente, reserve a cup of the starchy pasta cooking water, then drain the pasta and return it to the pot with the sauce. Toss until coated, adding a little cooking water to loosen, if necessary.
5. Plate and serve immediately with freshly grated Parmesan to taste.

Greengrocers' rigatoni

RIGATONI ALL'ORTOLANA

serves 6

This recipe derives its name, with neither contention nor complexity, from the simple fact that it is full of vegetables, much like a well-stocked greengrocer. Ultimately, *pasta all'ortolana* is one of those recipes that lends itself to a fridge raid. Truth be told, you can use more or less any vegetables you might have at your disposal to create a dish that is as munificently healthy as it is delicious. Aubergine must feature, however, if only for tradition's sake. Ensure you use good tomatoes, and don't forgo the garlic – these are key in such a simple recipe.

6 tbsp extra virgin olive oil
1 garlic clove, minced
½ fresh red chilli, seeds removed
*   and finely chopped*
2 courgettes, finely chopped
1 red pepper, finely chopped
1 large aubergine, finely chopped
100g cherry tomatoes, washed
*   and diced*
15g fresh basil leaves, finely chopped
750g rigatoni
50g Parmesan, or vegetarian
*   alternative, grated*
Salt, to taste

1. Heat the oil in a pan and sauté the garlic and chilli for 2 minutes.
2. Add the courgettes, red pepper and aubergine to the pan and sauté over a high heat for a couple of minutes. Cover with a lid, reduce the heat to medium and cook for 15 minutes.
3. Add the diced cherry tomatoes, salt and basil and stir together. Put the lid back on and cook for a further 2–3 minutes.
4. Bring a pot of generously salted water to the boil. Cook the pasta until al dente, following the packet instructions.
5. Once the pasta is al dente, drain and add to the sauce. Toss to coat, then add the grated Parmesan and sauté the pasta for another couple of minutes in the pan. Plate and serve immediately.

Pappardelle with wild mushrooms

PAPPARDELLE AL FUNGHI PORCINI

V/Ve

serves 2

The late Marcella Hazan, custodian of *cucina italiana* and one of Roberta's favourite food writers, once said that wild mushrooms were reason enough to visit Italy in the absence of any other. Those Italians lucky enough to live in the shadows of the country's Alps and Apennine Mountains would presumably agree, but they might be reluctant to shout quite so loudly about it.

You see, the wild mushrooms that sprout there, in particular the porcini variety found in the late summer and autumn, fetch a handsome price. So much so that mushroom picking has become a pastime, even a profession, in mountain communities. Those who seek out mushrooms for a living are named *fungaioli*. Tragically, their profession is fraught with danger; over the years, many *fungaioli* have perished while out picking the very mushrooms that had hitherto sustained them. This isn't due to the poisonous properties of imitator mushrooms (though amateurs are advised to exercise caution here), but rather countless hours spent scaling perilous mountains where the most precious specimens can be found.

40g unsalted butter

5 tbsp extra virgin olive oil

450g wild mushrooms of your choice, cleaned and sliced

200g porcini mushrooms (fresh or rehydrated, both work well)

1 garlic clove, minced

15–20g fresh parsley, chopped

40g Parmesan, or vegetarian alternative, grated, plus extra to serve

½ tsp sea salt flakes

1. Place the butter and oil in a pan over a medium heat. When the butter has melted, add the mushrooms and sauté over a medium-high heat for 3–4 minutes. Some mushrooms may exude natural moisture; continue to sauté gently until the water evaporates.

2. Add the garlic and fry for a minute or two. Add 100ml water (around half a glass) and leave to simmer on a low heat for 5–6 minutes, then stir through the parsley and season with salt and pepper.

3. Meanwhile, bring a pot of generously salted water to the boil. Cook the pasta until al dente, following the packet instructions.

4. Once the pasta is al dente, reserve half a cup of the starchy pasta cooking water, then drain the pasta and add it to the sauce. Toss to coat, adding the reserved cooking water to loosen the sauce, if needed.

5. Plate and serve immediately with freshly grated Parmesan to taste.

Spaghetti with crab, lemon & chilli

SPAGHETTI AL GRANCHIO, LIMONE E PEPERONCINO *serves 6*

We are firm believers that crab (*granchio* in Italian) is best served simply. This isn't because we are lazy (though we have our moments), but because the delicate flavour of crab lends itself to uncomplicated preparation. Serving high-quality fresh ingredients in a stripped back way is also a key tenet of the Italian culinary philosophy, which this recipe seems to encapsulate.

As crab is also a relatively expensive ingredient, accentuating its flavour with fresh lemon is the best way to go. Some recipes call for crab to be served in a tomato-based sauce, which strikes us as disrespectful to this special crustacean, whose subtle flavour can be lost to the tomatoes. Seaside eateries across Italy seem to share this view, serving crab simply with lemon and perhaps red chilli. So this recipe makes us think of summer holidays spent along the Italian coastline.

5 tbsp extra virgin olive oil
1 garlic clove, minced
1 fresh red chilli, seeds removed and finely chopped
350g white crab meat
100ml white wine
15g fresh parsley, finely chopped
750g spaghetti
Grated zest of 1 unwaxed lemon
Salt and black pepper, to taste

1. Heat the oil in a frying pan and cook the garlic and chilli over a low heat for 2 minutes until fragrant.
2. Add the crab meat and raise the heat slightly. Then add the wine and continue cooking for 3–4 minutes. If the sauce is too dry, add a little water. Stir through the chopped parsley.
3. Meanwhile, bring a pot of generously salted water to the boil. Cook the pasta until al dente, following the packet instructions.
4. Once the pasta is al dente, reserve a cup of the starchy pasta cooking water, then drain the pasta and add it to the pan with the crab. Toss to coat, and continue cooking on a low to medium heat, adding a little of the cooking water at a time until everything is nicely combined and glossy.
5. Add the lemon zest and toss to combine, then season with salt and black pepper. Plate and serve immediately.

Malloreddus with cavolo nero pesto

MALLOREDDUS AL PESTO DI CAVOLO NERO

serves 4

Also known as Tuscan kale, cavolo nero (literally 'black cabbage') has gained attention in recent years for its health-boosting credentials. Its black-green leaves, meanwhile, are a thing of almost funereal melodrama, as though they might have been dug up in the Addams Family's back garden.

This variety of kale didn't used to bask in such stardom, though. For centuries, cavolo nero was a staple crop of Tuscan peasants, being widely used in their *ribollita*, a bread stew from the region, as well as the classic minestrone. Regardless of its slightly faddy new-found fame, we love to use cavolo nero in this pesto. It is (happily) distinguished from other pestos by its robust flavour and Halloween-esque green.

*600g cavolo nero, washed and
    roughly chopped*
*100g Parmesan, or vegetarian
    alternative, grated, plus extra
    to serve*
45g pine nuts
*1–2 garlic cloves, peeled and cut
    in half*
70ml extra virgin olive oil
750g malloreddus
Salt, to taste

1. Bring a pot of generously salted water to the boil. Add the cavolo nero and cook for 3 minutes. Drain the cavolo nero and run under cold water to stop the cooking process and maintain its bright green colour. Squeeze out any excess water from the cavolo nero and set aside.

2. Place the Parmesan, pine nuts and garlic in a food processor. Blitz together until a rustic texture is achieved. Add the cavolo nero to the food processor with the olive oil and blitz again. If it's too thick, add a tablespoon of water and blend again. Add salt to taste.

3. Bring a pot of generously salted water to the boil. Cook the pasta until al dente, following the packet instructions.

4. Once the pasta is al dente, drain the pasta and return to the pot with the pesto. Toss to coat, then plate and serve immediately with freshly grated Parmesan to taste.

Pappardelle with saffron, pancetta & artichokes

PAPPARDELLE CON ZAFFERANO, PANCETTA
CROCCANTE E CARCIOFI

serves 6

Saffron is one of the few ingredients that, despite more than three millennia of documentation, continues to capture our collective imagination. It commands an air of mystery and intrigue, perhaps due to its enduring status as the world's most expensive spice. Ancient Rome was equally enthralled – whenever Emperor Nero returned to the imperial capital, strands of saffron would be cast upon the streets as a perfumed salutation. This seems unimaginably decadent: costing around $5,000 per kilo at the time of writing, one can scarcely imagine a modern politician being bestowed such a golden hello.

2 large artichokes, peeled
Juice of ½ unwaxed lemon
75ml double cream
5g saffron
40g Parmesan, grated,
  plus extra to serve
1 garlic clove, peeled and thinly
  sliced
5 tbsp extra virgin olive oil
100g pancetta, cubed
750g pappardelle
Salt and black pepper, to taste

1. Start by preparing the artichokes. Remove the hard outer leaves and the stem from each. Slice the artichokes in half, remove the choke (the hairy innards) and cut off the tips of the artichoke leaves. Slice these halves into smaller pieces. Soak the artichokes in water with the lemon juice for 5 minutes.

2. While the artichokes soak, bring a pan of generously salted water to the boil. Transfer the artichokes to the pan and cook for 10 minutes, then remove them with a slotted spoon and set aside, saving the cooking water for later use.

3. In a saucepan, gently heat the cream for around 2 minutes. Add the saffron and Parmesan, turn off the heat and stir to combine.

4. In a separate pan, sauté the garlic in the oil for 2 minutes until soft and translucent. Add the pancetta and fry until crispy, around 3–4 minutes. Add the sliced artichokes and sauté for 4–5 minutes. Remove any hard pieces of artichokes that remain.

5. Finally, add the saffron sauce to the artichokes and mix until fully incorporated.

6. Bring the artichoke cooking water to the boil. Cook the pasta until al dente, following the packet instructions. Once the pasta is al dente, drain the pasta and add to the sauce, tossing to coat. Season to taste.

7. Plate and serve immediately with freshly grated Parmesan to taste.

Spaghetti from Amatrice

SPAGHETTI ALL'AMATRICIANA

serves 2

The *all'amatriciana* sauce is often considered a staple of Roman cuisine, as it is ubiquitous in restaurants of the Italian capital. The people of Amatrice, more than 100 kilometres to the northeast, have a different opinion. For the Amatriciani, this is their dish, and one that should be protected at all costs. The acclaimed chef Carlo Cracco was even condemned by the deputy mayor of the town for his lapse of judgement after admitting to using garlic in his version. The magazine *Gambero Rosso* reported on 'the scandal of the garlic in the Amatriciana'. Cracco apologised, calling this an 'unpardonable' mistake.

In Rome, the *all'amatriciana* sauce is often served with bucatini, so much so that many now consider this pasta pairing established tradition. This is not actually the case. Spaghetti is the traditional pairing for the sauce and is the only pasta Amatriciani will endorse. Given their ferocity when it comes to protecting the traditions of their sauce, we have always been happy to oblige.

150g guanciale (if you really can't find it, opt for cubed pancetta)

1 fresh red chilli, seeds removed and finely chopped (use freshly cracked black pepper for a milder option)

400g quality tinned tomatoes, chopped

250g spaghetti

70g pecorino Romano, grated

Salt and black pepper, to taste

1. Remove and discard the tough rind of the guanciale, then cut the meat into cubes. Fry the cubes in a dry frying pan over a low heat for 6–7 minutes until crisp and browned. Once the fat renders, add the chilli and continue to fry for 2 minutes.
2. Add the tomatoes and crush them to create a rustic sauce. Allow this to simmer for at least 5 minutes so that it starts to thicken slightly before seasoning with salt and pepper.
3. Meanwhile, bring a pot of generously salted water to the boil. Cook the pasta until al dente, following the packet instructions.
4. Once the pasta is al dente, reserve a cup of the starchy pasta cooking water, then drain the pasta and add it to the sauce with the pecorino Romano, tossing until the spaghetti is completely coated. If necessary, add a splash of the cooking water to loosen the sauce. Plate and serve immediately.

Tagliatelle with walnut sauce

TAGLIATELLE AL SALSA DI NOCI

Many will be familiar with *pesto alla Genovese*, the classic green pesto from Genoa made with fresh basil and pine nuts. Despite being conceived in the same city, few know of its caffè-latte-coloured sibling, *salsa di noci*. This is true even within Italy. In any case, those who have tried this sauce agree that it is something of a gastronomic B-side to its better-known basil counterpart (this is no reflection of its beauty, merely its popularity). It's simple but incredibly elegant, highlighting the subtle flavour of walnuts by quietly featuring marjoram, garlic and a drop of milk. If you can find them, use Sorrento walnuts; we've found that they're the most delicious.

50g pine nuts
4 tbsp extra virgin olive oil
20g stale breadcrumbs
30g Parmesan, or vegetarian
 alternative, grated, plus extra
 to serve
1 garlic clove, peeled and halved
1 tsp dried marjoram
150g raw walnuts
100ml whole milk
500g tagliatelle
Salt, to taste

1. Place the pine nuts, olive oil, breadcrumbs, Parmesan, garlic, marjoram and salt in a mortar and grind with a pestle in a circular motion until a rugged paste is achieved.
2. Add the walnuts and continue grinding until combined, then transfer to a large bowl.
3. Heat the milk gently in a saucepan before adding to the bowl containing the pesto mixture. Do this gradually to control the consistency of the pesto. Mix until well combined, adding as much milk as is necessary to give a creamy yet textured sauce.
4. Bring a pot of generously salted water to the boil. Cook the pasta until al dente, following the packet instructions.
5. Once the pasta is al dente, reserve a cup of the starchy pasta cooking water, then drain the pasta and add it to the pesto. Toss to coat, adding a splash of the cooking water to loosen, if needed.
6. Plate and serve immediately with freshly grated Parmesan to taste.

Tips & Substitutions

- You could use a food processor in place of the pestle and mortar in this recipe. Pulse the ingredients roughly to preserve a rustic consistency.

Make your own
RAGÙ

Ragù is quite simply the Italian word for a meat-based sauce. Often, ragù is simmered for many hours, but this doesn't have to be the case if you're in a hurry. Many different regions of Italy have their own signature ragù, and we've included three of our favourite options here. By happy coincidence, each can be prepared in no more than 30 minutes. The base of celery, carrot and onion (known as a soffritto) is ever present in ragù recipes and provides an excellent way to put any of these leftover vegetables to use.

BASE RECIPE (SERVES 4)

- Choose your preferred additions from the regions opposite.
- Heat 3 tbsp olive oil in a pan over a medium-high heat.
- Add 50g finely chopped white or brown onion, 50g finely chopped celery and 50g finely diced carrot and cook for 3–4 minutes until softened.
- Add meat(s), as indicated in the options opposite, and begin to brown.
- Add 80ml white wine and allow to evaporate.
- Add salt and pepper to taste, 1 bay leaf, 500g tomato passata and allow to simmer for up to 30 minutes. Add a splash of water from time to time if the sauce becomes too thick.

Veneto

In step 3, add **350g finely chopped duck breast**. During step 5, add **1 clove** and **1 tsp ground cinnamon** along with the bay leaf. Serve the sauce with your choice of pasta and **Parmesan**.

Emilia-Romagna

Cook **150g diced pancetta** alongside the vegetables in step 2. In step 3, add **300g beef mince**. Serve the sauce with your choice of pasta and **Parmesan**.

Tuscany

In step 3, add **150g Italian sausage meat** and **300g beef mince**. In step 5, do not add the tomato passata and instead add **a sprig of fresh rosemary**. Serve the sauce with your choice of pasta and **Parmesan**.

Seafarer's spaghetti

SPAGHETTI ALLA MARINARA

serves 4

A recipe really wouldn't be Italian if its origins weren't in some way contentious, and, true to form, theories explaining the origins of the *salsa marinara* abound. Some claim this sauce – which in its simplest form can contain only tomatoes, oregano and garlic – was created by cooks on board ships returning from the New World. With a bounty of tomatoes suddenly at their disposal, or so the theory goes, these chefs of the high seas spent the return voyage creating new recipes, and the *salsa alla marinara* ('marino' being the Italian word for sailor) was, apparently, the result.

Others insist that the dish was actually created by the sailors' wives when their husbands returned from their voyages. Regardless of which theory floats your boat, what seems indivisible from the story of this sauce is the sea. And so, in tribute to it, our version includes anchovies, which melt down and dissolve into the sauce, leaving behind a mere whisper of the salty waters they came from.

6 tbsp extra virgin olive oil

1 garlic clove, peeled and sliced

4–5 anchovies, rinsed and roughly chopped

300g tomato passata

Dried oregano, to taste

750g spaghetti

15g fresh parsley, finely chopped

Pecorino Romano, grated, to serve

1. Heat the oil in a frying pan, add the garlic and fry for 2 minutes until golden, then add the anchovies and fry for another couple of minutes.
2. Add the passata and simmer for about 15 minutes, then add dried oregano to taste. Simmer gently for 10 minutes, then turn off the heat.
3. Meanwhile, bring a pot of generously salted water to the boil. Cook the pasta until al dente, following the packet instructions.
4. Once the pasta is al dente, reserve a cup of the starchy pasta cooking water, then drain the pasta and add it to the sauce. Toss to coat the spaghetti and continue cooking for about 2 more minutes. If the sauce is too dry, add a splash of the cooking water. Stir through the parsley.
5. Plate and serve immediately with freshly grated pecorino Romano to taste.

Tagliatelle with 'nduja, lemon & mascarpone

TAGLIATELLE 'NDUJA, LIMONE E MASCARPONE *serves 4*

Finn first ate this dish at a London restaurant, Padella, which specialises in fresh pasta. We were already serving a similar 'nduja sauce at Pasta Evangelists, which was lovely, but the addition of lemon and mascarpone was, to the credit of the Padella team, inspired.

'Nduja, for the uninitiated, is a spicy sausage from Calabria, made with the region's native chillies, and has a spreadable, pâté-like consistency, not dissimilar to Spain's sobrasada. The addition of mascarpone tempers its ferocious heat while transforming its deep red colour to a pretty coral. Sharp lemon cuts through the richness of both sausage and mascarpone, and we think it's just delicious.

500g tagliatelle
2 tbsp extra virgin olive oil
1 garlic clove, peeled and
   lightly crushed
120g 'nduja or sobrasada
300g mascarpone
50g Parmesan, grated,
   plus extra to serve
Juice and grated zest of
   1 unwaxed lemon
Salt and black pepper, to taste

1. Bring a pot of generously salted water to the boil. Cook the pasta until al dente, following the packet instructions. While the pasta cooks, prepare the sauce.
2. Heat a splash of oil in a large frying pan over a medium heat. Add the garlic to the pan and cook for 2 minutes until fragrant, then add the 'nduja and fry for a couple of minutes, helping the sausage to disintegrate with a fork. Remove the garlic from the pan and discard.
3. Reduce the heat and add the mascarpone, salt and pepper and a splash of the pasta cooking water. Stir to combine, then add the Parmesan and mix until creamy. Remove the sauce from the heat and stir through the lemon juice and zest.
4. Once the pasta is al dente, drain and toss with the sauce until coated.
5. Plate and serve immediately with freshly grated Parmesan to taste.

Spaghetti with wild garlic pesto

SPAGHETTI AL PESTO D'AGLIO SELVATICO

V/Ve

serves 4

Wild garlic has a sort of fairytale ring to it, as though it were part of some fabled woodland kingdom that humans cross into from time to time. In reality, the plant lives around us, abundantly, all year. Only its white flowers are ephemeral, appearing for a short period in the spring. Known as *erba orsina*, or 'the bear's herb' in Italian, some say the leaves were the first food enjoyed by bears waking from their winter slumber.

You'll be able to buy wild garlic flowers at farmers' markets, as well as online, usually between April and June. Much more rewarding, though, is to gather your own. It is found throughout the British Isles, and you can find information about where your nearest wild garlic plants are online. In London, for example, we've found wild garlic growing in a cemetery in Stoke Newington. This fragrant pesto, so evocative of springtime, was the happy result of our foraging.

150g wild garlic leaves, washed
50g blanched almonds
30g Parmesan, or vegetarian alternative, grated, plus extra to serve
30g pecorino Romano, or vegetarian alternative, grated
10g pine nuts
3 tbsp extra virgin olive oil
3 tbsp lemon juice
500g spaghetti
Salt, to taste

1. Place the wild garlic, almonds, Parmesan, pecorino Romano, pine nuts, olive oil and salt into a food processor and blitz until a creamy yet slightly chunky sauce is formed.
2. Transfer to a bowl and gradually add the lemon juice to the mixture, stirring to combine.
3. Bring a pot of generously salted water to the boil. Cook the pasta until al dente, following the packet instructions.
4. Once the pasta is al dente, reserve a cup of the starchy pasta cooking water, then drain the pasta and return it to the pot with the pesto. Toss until coated, adding a little cooking water to loosen, if necessary.
5. Plate and serve immediately with freshly grated Parmesan to taste

Woodsman's tagliatelle

PAPPARDELLE ALLA BOSCAIOLA

serves 4

The Italian word *boscaiola* refers to a 'woodsman' or 'lumberjack'. In this way, *pasta alla boscaiola* denotes pasta made in the manner of a woodsman – someone who spends their days in the shadows of the forests, emerging only as the sun sets to return to their homes. While many recipes for *pasta alla boscaiola* abound, one thing is certain: the mushroom is the protagonist of this woodland tale. And the porcini variety, found deep within the forests of central Italy, is particularly ubiquitous, if not ever-present, in *boscaiola* recipes.

5 tbsp extra virgin olive oil
1 garlic clove, minced
500g mixed wild mushrooms,
    cleaned and roughly chopped
80g salsiccia piccante
    (spicy sausage) or chorizo,
    roughly chopped
500g tomato passata
750g tagliatelle
15g fresh parsley, finely chopped
Salt and black pepper, to taste
Parmesan, to serve

1. Place the olive oil and garlic in a frying pan over a gentle heat, and cook for 2 minutes until the garlic is browned and fragrant, taking care not to burn it.
2. Add the mushrooms and sausage to the pan and sauté for 5 minutes, then add the passata and let the sauce simmer for 20 minutes.
3. In the meantime, bring a pot of generously salted water to the boil. Cook the pasta until al dente, following the packet instructions.
4. Once the pasta is al dente, drain and add to the sauce, tossing to coat. Add the parsley and black pepper and mix to combine.
5. Plate and serve immediately with freshly grated Parmesan to taste.

Orecchiette with red pesto from Sicily

ORECCHIETTE CON PESTO ALLA TRAPANESE

On the Mediterranean's largest island, Sicily, the arrival of springtime is heralded by the blossoming of almond trees. Those who have visited the region will recall their beauty: a vision of pink-white flowers that enrapture the islanders anew each year. This tradition is akin to Japan's hanami, or 'flower viewing', when locals enjoy the transient beauty of their islands' similar-looking cherry blossoms.

The people of Sicily don't just admire the trees, though. Their fruit, the almond nut, is used extensively in *cucina siciliana*. Centuries ago, when sailors from the Republic of Genoa docked in the island's ports, particularly Trapani, their traditional *agliata* sauce (made from garlic and walnuts, the precursor for *Salsa di Noci*, see page 113) was adapted to make use of the island's bountiful almonds and tomatoes. Most versions of the resultant *pesto alla Trapanese* call for fresh tomatoes, but we prefer the deep flavour of sun-dried tomatoes, another staple of the island.

½ garlic clove, roughly chopped
½ tsp sea salt flakes
40g blanched almonds
200g sun-dried tomatoes
50g fresh basil leaves, roughly torn
50ml extra virgin olive oil
20g pecorino Romano, or vegetarian
   alternative, grated, plus extra
   to serve
500g orecchiette

1. Place the garlic and salt in a mortar and grind with a pestle in a circular motion until a paste is formed. Add the almonds and pound and grind the mixture until the nuts are broken down and incorporated.

2. Add the sun-dried tomatoes and basil and continue to grind to combine. Gradually add the oil and pecorino Romano, grinding until well combined and creamy.

3. Bring a pot of generously salted water to the boil. Cook the pasta until al dente, following the packet instructions.

4. Once the pasta is al dente, reserve a cup of the starchy pasta cooking water, then drain the pasta and return it to the pot with the pesto. Toss until coated, adding a little cooking water to loosen, if necessary.

5. Plate and serve immediately with freshly grated pecorino Romano to taste.

Tips & Substitutions

- You could use a food processor in place of the pestle and mortar in this recipe. Pulse the ingredients roughly to preserve a rustic consistency.

Tagliatelle with porcini & black truffle

TAGLIATELLE AL PORCINI E TARTUFO NERO

This recipe celebrates two of northern and central Italy's most prized ingredients: the porcini mushroom and the black truffle. Both of these specimens are unearthed with great difficulty yet promise great rewards, particularly when brought together, as here. While the sprouting of funghi porcini tends not to coincide with Italy's summer truffle season, both ingredients are available year-round in preserved forms. Dried porcini mushrooms, for example, are fantastic, and we're very happy to source preserved truffles from our friends at Truffle Hunter, whose online shop is to die for. Both ingredients are wonderful, earthy and bring a touch of indulgence to any table they're served at.

3 tbsp extra virgin olive oil

500g porcini mushrooms,
   cleaned and sliced

2 garlic cloves, peeled and
   lightly crushed

15g fresh parsley, finely chopped,
   plus extra to serve

750g tagliatelle

70ml vegetable broth

Salt, to taste

25–30g black truffle, shaved

1. Place the olive oil in a pan over a medium heat. Add the mushrooms, garlic and parsley and sauté for 3 to 5 minutes, until the mushrooms are slightly softened.

2. Place half the mushrooms in a food processor and purée until creamy. Return this purée to the pan containing the rest of the mushrooms.

3. Bring a pot of generously salted water to the boil. Cook the pasta until al dente, following the packet instructions.

4. Once the pasta is al dente, drain and add to the pan with the mushroom sauce. Dilute with a couple of tablespoons of vegetable broth and continue to cook for a couple of minutes over a low heat.

5. Toss the mixture until well combined. If necessary, add a couple more tablespoons of broth to loosen the mixture. Add the parsley and shaved truffle, then plate and serve immediately.

Rigatoni with tuna

RIGATONI AL TONNO

In the UK, canned tuna has a bit of a bad reputation. Finn remembers being packed off to school with tuna mayonnaise sandwiches, while the memory of tuna vol-au-vents at 1970s' dinner parties remains inescapable for many. Italians, however, have no such qualms about tinned tuna, perhaps precisely because tuna mayonnaise was never a hit in Italy. Instead, tuna (*tonno* in Italian) is widely enjoyed across the country, with both its fresh and tinned varieties equally respected. This is particularly true in Sicily, where the historical *mattanza*, the island's annual massacre of tuna (which has fortunately ceased), has left a legacy of the fish being a staple of the Sicilian diet.

Don't be tempted to use tuna in spring water, or even brine, in this recipe, as the fish is invariably bone dry. If you can, opt instead for a high-quality tuna from sustainable sources in oil.

6 tbsp extra virgin olive oil

1 small red onion, finely chopped

25g capers, rinsed

35g Taggiasche olives, pitted and roughly chopped

220g quality tuna in oil

15g fresh parsley, finely chopped, plus extra to serve

700g fresh yellow tomatoes, washed and roughly chopped

500g rigatoni

Salt and black pepper, to taste

1 tsp chilli oil, to serve (optional)

1. Heat the oil in a frying pan and cook the onion for 4 minutes until golden. Add the capers, olives and tuna and cook for 2 minutes, then stir in the parsley.
2. Add the chopped tomatoes, season with salt and pepper and let simmer for 10–15 minutes until thick and glossy.
3. Meanwhile, bring a pot of generously salted water to the boil. Cook the pasta until al dente, following the packet instructions.
4. Once the pasta is al dente, reserve a cup of the starchy pasta cooking water, then drain the pasta and add to the sauce. Toss to coat, adding a splash of cooking water if needed to ensure the sauce coats the pasta fully.
5. Plate and serve immediately, finished with a drizzle of chilli oil, if desired.

Tagliatelle with ham & leek

TAGLIATELLE SPECK E PORRO   *serves 6*

As Finn and Roberta have both spent time living in Austria, they have an affinity for some of the cuisine enjoyed in the Alps, along the border between Austria and Italy. From *Schlutzkrapfen*, a German-named variety of filled pasta, to *Spätzle*, a sort of Germanic gnocchi, the foods originating in the bitterly cold region of South Tyrol, split between the two countries, tend to be hearty and warming. Speck is our favourite. While *Speck* is the German word for 'bacon', on the Italian side of the border it also denotes a specific type of *prosciutto* that, under European law, can only be produced in South Tyrol. It has an unmistakable smoky flavour that we find utterly wonderful. If you can find it, great. If not, *prosciutto di Parma*, equally wonderful, albeit in other ways, will work just as well.

50g unsalted butter
1 large leek, cleaned and sliced
3 tbsp extra virgin olive oil, plus
    extra to serve
1 vegetable stock cube
750g tagliatelle
150g speck, cubed
Parmesan, grated, to serve

1. Melt the butter in a frying pan, then add the leeks and 2 tablespoons of the olive oil and sweat the leeks for 5 minutes until softened.
2. Crumble the vegetable stock cube into the pan, add a splash of water and cook for about 15 minutes, until the leeks are completely soft, adding more water as needed.
3. Transfer the leeks to a food processor and purée until creamy.
4. In a separate pan, fry the speck in the remaining oil for 2–3 minutes over a medium-high heat until crispy.
5. Bring a pot of generously salted water to the boil. Cook the pasta until al dente, following the packet instructions.
6. Once the pasta is al dente, reserve a cup of the starchy pasta cooking water, then drain the pasta and add to the pan with the speck, along with the leek sauce. Toss to coat, adding a splash of cooking water if necessary, to ensure the sauce completely coats the pasta.
7. Plate and serve immediately with freshly grated Parmesan and a drizzle of olive oil to taste.

Spaghetti with black olive pesto

SPAGHETTI CON PESTO DI OLIVE NERE

serves 6

Many people – Finn included – say they prefer green olives, or even a life without olives. Yet they love this recipe when they taste it. We appreciate that it requires a leap of faith, particularly as the darkness of the pesto lacks beauty. But stay with us here.

For starters, although this recipe seems far-removed from the familiar *pesto alla Genovese* (see page 88), this is actually not so. In fact, the Taggiasche olives that Roberta likes here are the same olives used in Liguria – home of pesto – to produce Ligurian extra virgin olive oil. In turn, this oil – at least within the region – is used to prepare the famous basil pesto. The Taggiasche variety of olive also has a less acidic, sweeter character than other black olives, which makes for a gentler pesto than you might imagine. If you can, give it a go – you might just be converted to the dark side.

10g fresh basil leaves, roughly torn
120g blanched almonds
70g Taggiasche olives, pitted and
*   roughly chopped*
5 tbsp extra virgin olive oil, plus
*   extra to serve*
40g pecorino Romano, or vegetarian
*   alternative, grated, plus extra*
*   to serve*
750g spaghetti

1. Put the basil and almonds in a food processor and give them a quick blitz. Add the olives and blitz until a rough texture is achieved.
2. Add half the olive oil to the food processor with the pecorino Romano and blitz again.
3. Finally, drizzle in the remaining oil and blitz until you reach the desired consistency. You may require slightly more oil. Avoid overblending, however, as a rustic texture is preferred.
4. Bring a pot of generously salted water to the boil. Cook the pasta until al dente, following the packet instructions.
5. Once the pasta is al dente, reserve a cup of the starchy pasta cooking water, then drain the pasta and return it to the pan. Stir through the pesto, adding a splash of the reserved cooking water, if necessary, to ensure the pesto completely coats the pasta.
6. Plate and serve immediately with a drizzle of olive oil and freshly grated pecorino Romano to taste.

PART 3

30 MINUTES

It takes minimal effort, and just a little time, to coax an astonishing level of flavour from some of the core ingredients of the Italian pantry. Half an hour seems a short period when held up against many people's commutes, or hours spent gazing at the screens of our smartphones. But it provides ample opportunity to brown morsels of fennel sausage meat or create tiny polpettine (miniature meatballs) in the palm of your hand. Chubby cubes of aubergine can be roasted, taking on an earthy flavour, or Roberta's beloved cime di rapa (turnip tops) boiled down into their bitter submission. In this way, affording yourself an extra 10 or 20 minutes to prepare a dish than you might otherwise can open many doors, for this small amount of additional time allows new ingredients and flavours to enter the fold.

It isn't all about flavour, though. As we have already seen, some of the most flavoursome dishes can indeed be prepared in a matter of minutes. To create certain textures – an equally important dimension in cooking – can take a little longer. Turning a high heat down to a low simmer allows us to revel in the creamy texture of lentils, for example, as they are given the opportunity to truly relax into a sauce. A bit of extra time will also allow the opportunity to fry certain ingredients, like the courgettes in our Spaghetti from Nerano (see page 169) with its origins in the sunny Sorrento peninsula.

With the addition of fresh herbs for aromatic depth, spices for warmth and capers or anchovies for a salty kick, the possibilities are endless – but many of these ingredients beg to be given a little longer to impart their flavour profiles. In this section, we are happy to oblige, not least because setting aside 30 minutes can be a wholly uplifting experience, particularly after a long day at work, when a bit of light chopping and quiet simmering in a fairy-lit kitchen is, at least for us, a cathartic release. Pour yourself a glass of wine and breathe, inhaling the aromas along the way.

Spaghetti with mini meatballs

SPAGHETTI CON POLPETTINE DI CARNE

serves 4

While spaghetti with meatballs is often deemed to be of American extraction, this isn't entirely the case. In fact, nonne across Italy are widely known to prepare polpettine, particularly for their grandchildren's pleasure. Polpettine are dinky meatballs. They are quite different from their oversized American counterparts, and the small hands of children are particularly deft at forming these, so if you have access to child labour, this resource comes heartily recommended. We promise they'll enjoy themselves too.

500g beef mince
1 medium egg
30g Parmesan, grated,
  plus extra to serve
60ml whole milk
15–20g fresh parsley,
  finely chopped
70g breadcrumbs
3 tbsp extra virgin olive oil
½ brown or white onion,
  finely chopped
½ carrot, finely chopped
100ml good red wine
600g tomato passata
500g spaghetti
Salt, to taste

1. Put the beef mince, egg, Parmesan, milk, chopped parsley and a pinch of salt into a large bowl, and knead well with a fork until you have a homogeneous mixture. Gradually add the breadcrumbs, continuing to knead until well incorporated.

2. Form the meatballs by rolling small amounts of the mixture between your hands – aim for around 18–20 meatballs in total. Place the meatballs on a parchment-lined tray.

3. Heat the oil in a large saucepan over a medium heat. Add the onion and carrot and fry for 3–4 minutes until they start to soften, stirring continuously.

4. Gradually add the meatballs, cooking for a few minutes until they are browned on all sides. Add the red wine and cook for 3 minutes, then add the passata and 50ml water. Stir until well mixed, cover with a lid and simmer for 25 minutes, stirring occasionally.

5. While the sauce is cooking, bring a pot of generously salted water to the boil. Cook the pasta until al dente, following the packet instructions.

6. Once the pasta is al dente, reserve a cup of the starchy pasta cooking water, then drain the pasta.

7. When the sauce is ready, add the pasta, tossing until well combined. If necessary, add a little of the cooking water to loosen the sauce.

8. Plate and serve immediately with freshly grated Parmesan to taste.

Gnocchi with asparagus sauce

GNOCCHI CON SALSA DI ASPARAGI

serves 6

We have several friends from Sardinia and so visit the island a couple of times a year. When you get out of Cagliari and into the countryside, you'll find some of the healthiest – and happiest – people in the world. Sardinia is one of five 'Blue Zones', where some of the longest-living populations of our planet can be found. Our guess is that the abundance of fresh vegetables available on the island has something to do with it.

Asparagus, in particular, has grown in the wild there for hundreds of years, delighting the islanders anew when it comes into season each spring. Caution must be taken, though: the asparagus plant is prickly and puts up a good fight. We find the duel with nature to be worth it, as the freshness and flavour of Sardinia's wild asparagus is incomparable. Having said that, we made this sauce with standard farmed asparagus when we got back to London and it was more than delightful. You needn't serve it with gnocchi, either, if you aren't a fan; pasta is just as good a pairing here.

450g asparagus spears, washed
30g unsalted butter
1 shallot, finely chopped
250ml double cream
500g gnocchi
Salt and white pepper, to taste

1. Cut the tips off the asparagus spears and chop the remaining stems into bite-sized pieces. Finely slice the tips and set aside for later, as these will be your garnish.
2. Melt the butter in a large frying pan over a medium heat. Add the shallot and gently fry for 2 minutes until translucent. Add the chopped asparagus stems and cook for a further 3 minutes.
3. Add a pinch of salt and freshly ground white pepper, then sprinkle with a splash of water. Cover the pan and continue to cook over a medium heat for around 20 minutes, stirring occasionally.
4. Add the cream and continue to cook, stirring continuously with a wooden spoon. Allow the mixture to reduce until you are left with a thick, creamy sauce.
5. While the sauce finishes cooking, bring a pot of generously salted water to the boil and cook the gnocchi, following the packet instructions. Transfer the cooked gnocchi to the asparagus cream sauce and toss well to coat.
6. Plate and serve immediately, garnished with the finely sliced asparagus tips.

Rigatoni with Sicily's fennel sausage

RIGATONI CON SALSICCIA E FINOCCHIETTO   *serves 6*

We know that fennel is divisive. But please have faith, for this dish will reward it handsomely. Fennel is sublime with sausage and an eminently Sicilian ingredient. In fact, the herb flourishes spontaneously across the island, but particularly in and around the mountains, resulting in it being known as *finocchio di montagna*, or mountain fennel. You'll know you've arrived in Sicily when you detect its anise-like fragrance in the warm island air.

The herb and (importantly) its seeds are harvested by the islanders during spring and the early days of summer. While the fresh fronds of wild fennel must be used within a matter of days before they perish, the seeds are dried in the abundant Sicilian sunshine and can be used throughout the year. In this recipe, we celebrate fennel in both forms. Sicilians love to eat fennel with Italian sausage as, in a similar way to sage, the herb has a fantastic ability to accentuate the savoury flavour of the sausage meat. For a similar sauce from the neighbouring island of Sardinia (but *rosso*, made with tomatoes), see Malloreddus with Sausage Ragù from Sardinia (see page 187).

2 tbsp olive oil
900g Italian sausage meat
  (ideally infused with fennel)
1 large brown or white onion,
  finely chopped
120g fennel with tops, chopped
1 tsp fennel seeds, roughly ground
1 fresh red chilli, finely chopped
1 garlic clove, minced
80ml white wine
100ml chicken stock
750g rigatoni
400ml single cream
Salt and black pepper, to taste

1. Heat the olive oil in a large pan over a medium heat. Add the sausage meat, using a fork or wooden spatula to break the meat into small pieces, and fry for around 10 minutes, until the sausage is nicely browned.
2. Add the onion, fennel (not the fennel tops), fennel seeds, chilli and garlic, and fry for a further 15 minutes.
3. Add the wine, allowing the mixture to cook until the alcohol evaporates. Then pour in the stock, season with salt and pepper, cover the pan with a lid and simmer gently for 30 minutes.
4. After 30 minutes, stir the cream and fennel tops into the sauce.
5. While the sauce is cooking, bring a pot of generously salted water to the boil. Cook the pasta until al dente, following the packet instructions.
6. Once the pasta is al dente, reserve a cup of the starchy pasta cooking water, then drain the pasta. Add the pasta to the sauce, tossing until well combined, and adding a drop of the cooking water to loosen the sauce, if needed.
7. Plate and serve immediately, finishing the dish with more freshly cracked black pepper.

Orecchiette with roasted pepper sauce

ORECCHIETTE CON SALSA DI PEPERONI ARROSTITI

V/Ve

serves 4

For us, this recipe is emblematic of Italy's approach to cooking. Where the recipes of some cuisines around the world prescribe long lists of ingredients, some of them esoteric and a real challenge to find, many Italian dishes have scarcely more than a handful of ingredients – and seem so much better for it. This sauce is a case in point and requires just five ingredients.

One drawback of Italy's stripped-back approach, though, is that there is often no place to hide, and a dish can live or die based on the quality of the underlying ingredients. When picking your peppers and tomatoes, bear this in mind and take care to choose the best specimens you can find. The San Marzano tomato, which grows in the volcanic soils of Mount Vesuvius, is fantastic here, and is becoming increasingly easy to find in the UK nowadays, and certainly online. They have lots of sweet, thick flesh and relatively few seeds, making them perfect for use in sauces featuring tomatoes.

3 red peppers
4 tbsp extra virgin olive oil
500g tomatoes, (ideally the
*   San Marzano variety)*
2 tsp sea salt flakes
500g orecchiette
15g fresh basil leaves, finely shredded
Freshly ground black pepper, to taste

1. Preheat your oven to 200°C. Halve the red peppers, removing the core and seeds, before placing on a roasting tray and drizzling with a tablespoon of olive oil. Season with salt and pepper and place in the oven for around 20 minutes, or until softened and slightly charred.

2. While the peppers are roasting, heat the remaining oil in a large saucepan over a medium-high heat. Add the tomatoes to the pan with 2 teaspoons of salt and fry gently until the peppers have finished cooking.

3. At the same time, bring a pot of generously salted water to the boil. Cook the pasta until al dente, following the packet instructions. Once the pasta is al dente, drain and set aside.

4. Remove the peppers from the oven and leave them to cool for a couple of minutes. Once cool enough to handle, remove as much of the skin as possible and discard. Roughly chop the remaining flesh and add to the pan of tomatoes with freshly grated black pepper to season. Crush the mixture gently using a potato masher or wooden spoon.

5. Once the sauce appears thick and shiny, add the pasta to the sauce and stir to combine. Remove from the heat and add the fresh basil, then serve immediately.

Seafood spaghetti

SPAGHETTI AL FRUTTI DI MARE

The Italian term *frutti di mare* ('seafood' or 'fruits of the sea') seems to encapsulate how Italians feel about seafood. It's something special: a treasure bestowed by the oceans on the people walking the land. This reverence has been seen on the Italian peninsula for millennia, since the days of Ancient Rome, where nobles are said to have feasted on lobster, octopus, clams, mussels, and more. With one of the world's longest coastlines, this voracious appetite for seafood lives on in modern Italy, just as it does in our homes in the UK.

This is Roberta's favourite seafood recipe, bringing together an assortment of her favourite *frutti di mare*. Whenever we prepare this, with fresh, tentacled squid and beautiful mussels in their purple-veined shells, we can't help but feel like we're reconnecting with our primeval ancestors.

*400g clams, soaked in plenty of
    water for 1 hour*
*700g mussels in shells, rinsed
    and de-bearded*
4 tbsp extra virgin olive oil
*1 garlic clove, peeled and
    lightly crushed*
1 fresh red chilli, cut in half
300g squid, cut into 1cm thick rings
175ml white wine
60g cherry tomatoes, halved
500g spaghetti
400g shell-on raw king prawns
15g fresh parsley, chopped roughly
Salt, to taste

1. Place a pan with a lid over a medium-high heat. Once hot, add the clams and mussels along with 2 tablespoons of water. Put the lid on the pan and cook for 4 minutes.
2. Once cooked, strain the flavoursome cooking liquid through a tea strainer or muslin cloth and set aside. Put the pan with the clams and mussels to one side too. Discard any mussels that haven't opened.
3. Set a separate frying pan over a medium-high heat and warm the oil. Once hot, add the garlic clove and chilli and allow them to infuse the oil for a minute or two until fragrant. Remove the garlic and chilli from the pan and discard.
4. Add the squid to the pan and cook for 3–4 minutes, then add the white wine and the liquid set aside from cooking the clams and mussels. Cook over a low heat for 10 minutes, adding the cherry tomatoes and salt a minute or two before the end of the cooking time.
5. Meanwhile, bring a pot of generously salted water to the boil. Cook the pasta until al dente, following the packet instructions.
6. After cooking the squid and tomatoes for 10 minutes, add the prawns, mussels and clams and cook for a further 4 minutes until the prawns change colour.
7. Drain the spaghetti and add to the pan with the seafood. Sprinkle over the fresh parsley and serve immediately.

Pappardelle with white ragù

PAPPARDELLE AL RAGÙ BIANCO

serves 4

Roberta first ate *ragù bianco*, literally 'white ragù', on a trip to Tuscany many years ago. Although similar versions exist in the south, these always include tomatoes – a red, or *rosso*, ragù. In Tuscany, white ragù is most often – and traditionally – served with pici, which resembles thick, oversized spaghetti and is made from merely flour and water. Any long pasta shape – spaghetti or tagliatelle, for example – is fantastic here though. Roberta particularly likes pappardelle, which does a fantastic job of sopping up this sauce.

Traditionally, only beef is used to prepare a *ragù bianco*. Some variations call for pork to be added, and others even chicken, which is rarely found in traditional pasta dishes. In any case, for sheer flavour, if not tradition, Roberta likes to add a bit of Italian sausage when preparing this dish at home in the UK. It's a favourite of ours on a dark winter evening, made with love to warm the cockles of your heart.

4 tbsp extra virgin olive oil

½ brown or white onion, finely chopped

1 celery stick, finely chopped

1 carrot, finely chopped

450g beef mince

150g Italian sausage meat (ideally infused with fennel), crumbled

1 tbsp cornflour

100ml white wine

400ml beef broth

2 bay leaves

750g pappardelle

Salt and black pepper, to taste

Parmesan, to serve

Chilli oil, to serve

1. Heat 3 tablespoons of oil in a saucepan and fry the onion, celery and carrot for about 1 minute. Add the beef mince and sausage, using a fork or wooden spatula to break the sausage meat into small pieces, and cook for a few minutes until lightly browned. Add the cornflour and stir through.

2. Increase the heat to high and continue to cook, stirring often. Gradually add the white wine, letting it evaporate before adding the beef broth and bay leaves. Once the sauce is boiling, reduce the heat to low, cover the pot with a lid and leave to simmer for at least 20 minutes. The white ragù should have thickened and reached a creamy consistency. Season with salt and pepper to taste and add the remaining tablespoon of olive oil.

3. While the sauce is cooking, bring a pot of generously salted water to the boil. Cook the pasta until al dente, following the packet instructions. Once the pasta is al dente, drain and add to the ragù, stirring over a low heat for a couple of minutes.

4. Plate and serve immediately with freshly grated Parmesan and chilli oil to taste.

Baked rigatoni from Trani

RIGATONI AL FORNO ALLA TRANESE

V/Ve

serves 6

Some 40 kilometres along the coast from Bari, the regional capital of Puglia, you'll find the white-washed seaport of Trani. Roberta, who comes from the region, has happy memories of visiting the town as a little girl, and has returned many times since. Along with the neighbouring communities of Andria and Barletta, Trani is often called the 'Pearl of the Adriatic' in appreciation of its architecture. You'll find a mélange of Romanesque, Norman and Byzantine influences here, owing to the subjugation of Puglia by many different masters from foreign kingdoms.

Although Trani's buildings are beautiful indeed, Roberta gets far more excited about the dish this port town gives its name to. *Pasta al forno alla tranese*, now a staple of Apulian cuisine more widely, is one of her favourite recipes. *Stracciatella di bufala*, a fresh cheese from the region, is traditional here, but you can substitute *mozzarella di bufala* with confidence should you struggle to find it. Burrata, whose oozing core is in any case made up of stracciatella, would also be a good choice.

2 tbsp extra virgin olive oil,
*   plus extra to drizzle*
1 brown or white onion, finely
*   chopped*
800g tomato passata
400g cherry tomatoes, quartered
10g fresh basil leaves, roughly torn
1 garlic clove, minced
750g rigatoni
120g pecorino Romano,
*   or vegetarian alternative,*
*   grated*
200g stracciatella
35g breadcrumbs
Salt, to taste

1. Preheat the oven to 180°C.
2. Heat the oil in a pan over a medium heat, then add the onion and cook for around 5 minutes. Pour in the passata and cook for another 10 minutes.
3. In a bowl, mix the tomatoes with the basil, garlic and salt to taste. Set aside.
4. Bring a pot of generously salted water to the boil. Cook the pasta for half the time instructed on the packet, as it will cook further in the oven. Drain the pasta and add to the pan of sauce.
5. Add half the tomato mixture to the pan with 100g of the pecorino Romano and mix thoroughly.
6. Pour half of the rigatoni into a 30cm square baking dish or lasagne dish and top with the stracciatella. Cover with the remaining pasta, then add the remaining tomato mixture and pecorino Romano, and the breadcrumbs. Finish with a drizzle of extra virgin olive oil.
7. Bake in the oven for 10 minutes, until the tomatoes and cheese are nicely browned and the pasta is cooked. Plate and serve immediately.

Black sea spaghetti

SPAGHETTI AL NERO DI SEPPIA   *serves 6*

In this edible melodrama, *nero di seppia* is the protagonist. Literally 'black of the cuttlefish', it is the obsidian-coloured ink produced beneath the waves by this mysterious mollusc. We love cooking with it, and not merely because it plunges all that it touches into theatrical darkness.

As is understood well by the chefs of Venice, where *risotto al nero di seppia* is widely enjoyed, cuttlefish ink also imparts a subtle flavour in its own right. This flavour, we can reassure you, is neither strong nor overpowering, as the ink's enveloping blackness might suggest. Instead, it's more of a salty flavour: a taste of brine. For us, it's a lingering whisper of the ocean the cuttlefish came from, spiriting us away to the Venetian seaside.

500g cuttlefish, ink sacs included
4 tbsp extra virgin olive oil
1 shallot, finely sliced
1 garlic clove, peeled and lightly crushed
100ml white wine
1 tsp tomato paste
1 fresh red chilli, seeds removed and finely chopped
750g spaghetti
Handful of fresh parsley, finely chopped, to serve
Salt, to taste

1. Remove the skin from the cuttlefish, reserving the ink sacs for later use. Alternatively, ask your fishmonger for prepared cuttlefish, but be sure to ask for ink sacs as well. Rinse the cuttlefish several times under cold running water. Separate the tentacles from the ink sacs before cutting the body of the cuttlefish into 1cm strips. Freeze the tentacles for the next time you make calamari.

2. Heat the oil in a pot over a medium heat and add the shallot and garlic clove. Fry for a couple of minutes, then add the cuttlefish and white wine and increase the heat until the alcohol evaporates, then lower the heat and cook the cuttlefish for about 10 minutes.

3. In a small bowl, combine the tomato paste with a ladleful of hot water and a small pinch of salt. Remove and discard the garlic from the cuttlefish pan, and add the dissolved tomato paste and chilli. Continue cooking for 10–15 minutes over a low heat.

4. Meanwhile, bring a pot of generously salted water to the boil. Cook the pasta until al dente, following the packet instructions.

5. Complete the sauce by adding the black cuttlefish ink. Use a pair of scissors to pierce the ink sac, decanting the contents directly into the sauce. Stir and cook for 3 minutes – you are aiming for a thick sauce with a deep, black colour.

6. Once the pasta is al dente, drain and add to the sauce. Plate, top with the parsley and serve immediately.

Tagliatelle with sea bass

TAGLIATELLE AL BRANZINO

The region of Tuscany is best known for its rich, meat-based ragù dishes, notably Wild Boar Ragù (see page 206). Less well known, but no less fantastic, are the dishes of its coastline and lagoons. In the municipalities of Monte Argentario and Ortebello, squished into the far southern corner of Tuscany along the Tyrrhenian Sea, it's more common to find *spigola*, or sea bass, on restaurant menus than Tuscany's iconic wild boar. This is because the lagoon of Ortebello, eponymous with the pretty settlement on its shores, is replete with the fish. The munificent waters sustain and delight the locals in equal measure, and have done for thousands of years.

2 tbsp extra virgin olive oil
1 garlic clove, peeled and
    lightly crushed
1 fresh red chilli, cut in half
300g cherry tomatoes, diced
100ml dry white wine
800g sea bass fillets, skin removed
    and flesh roughly chopped
15–20g fresh parsley, finely chopped,
    plus extra to serve
500g tagliatelle
Salt and black pepper, to taste

1. Place the oil in a large frying pan over a medium heat. Once hot, add the garlic and the chilli and fry for a couple of minutes until golden and fragrant. Remove the garlic and chilli from the pan and discard.
2. Add the tomatoes to the oil and cook for around 5 minutes.
3. Deglaze the pan with the white wine, and once the alcohol has evaporated completely, add the sea bass chunks and parsley. Continue cooking for 5–10 minutes until the fish is completely white, stirring continuously so the delicate fish doesn't stick to the pan.
4. Bring a pot of generously salted water to the boil. Cook the pasta until al dente, following the packet instructions.
5. Once the pasta is al dente, reserve a cup of the starchy pasta cooking water, then drain the pasta and add to the sauce. Toss until the pasta is completely coated, adding a little of the cooking water to loosen the sauce, if needed.
6. Plate and serve immediately, garnished with extra parsley.

Orecchiette with broccoli & chilli pesto

ORECCHIETTE AL PESTO DI BROCCOLI E PEPERONCINO   *serves 4*

This is one of those dishes we love to eat when, after a few too many glasses of Prosecco the night before, the body cries out for green invigoration. Broccoli, which was first cultivated on the Italian peninsula more than two millennia ago, is a staple of the Mediterranean diet and is distinguished by its long list of health-giving minerals and vitamins, particularly vitamins C and D. Where possible, always steam (or even microwave) broccoli, as boiling the vegetable diminishes its beneficial properties.

Having said all that, we should emphasise that, though incredibly good for you, we eat this because it is a delicious pick-me-up, not because it is a 'health food'. The chilli in this recipe does not make the pesto hot, per se; it merely adds a kick which is sometimes just what the doctor ordered. For an entirely plant-based version, simply leave out the pecorino, but do add extra salt to compensate.

600g broccoli
10–15g fresh basil leaves,
    roughly torn
40g pecorino Romano, or vegetarian
    alternative, grated, plus extra
    to serve
25g blanched almonds
35g pine nuts
1 fresh red chilli, seeds removed
    and roughly chopped
2 tsp sea salt flakes
100ml extra virgin olive oil
500g orecchiette

1. Cut the hard stalk off the broccoli, discard, and separate the florets into individual pieces. Steam the broccoli for around 7 minutes, then transfer immediately to a bowl of iced water, preventing further cooking and preserving its green colour.

2. Drain the broccoli and dry well with kitchen paper. Place in a food processor with the basil, pecorino Romano, almonds, pine nuts, chilli and salt. Gradually drizzle the oil into the mixture, pulsing between each addition until a rugged sauce is formed.

3. Bring a pot of generously salted water to the boil. Cook the pasta until al dente, following the packet instructions.

4. Once the pasta is al dente, reserve a cup of the starchy pasta cooking water, then drain the pasta.

5. Return it to the pan, along with the broccoli pesto, and toss until the pasta is completely coated, adding a splash of the cooking water to loosen the pesto, if needed.

6. Plate and serve immediately with freshly grated pecorino Romano to taste.

Rigatoni with Genovese sauce

RIGATONE CON RAGÙ GENOVESE   *serves 4*

Quite bizarrely, pasta served with 'Genovese' sauce comes not from the port of Genoa, but from Naples, some several hundred kilometres south. It's said the sauce takes its name from Genovese sailors, who, hailing from the Republic of Genoa, would dock in the port of Naples. To this day, this fact remains a source of bemusement not just for tourists to the region but also Italians, many of whom assume the sauce must, given its name, come from Genoa.

Like many sauces from the Italian repertoire, *ragù Genovese* begins with a simple soffritto of celery, carrot and onion. What distinguishes *ragù Genovese*, however, is its disproportionate use of onion in the soffritto. As the vast quotient of onion caramelises, it lends a slight sweetness to the ragù that Neapolitans adore.

700g brown or white onions, finely chopped (you may wish to do this in a food processor given the volume)
1 tsp white wine vinegar
6 tbsp olive oil
1 celery stick, julienned
1 carrot, julienned
600g beef mince
100ml white wine
2 bay leaves
500g rigatoni
Salt and black pepper, to taste
Parmesan, grated, to serve

1. Soak the chopped onions for 10 minutes in salted water with the white wine vinegar.
2. While the onions soak, heat the oil in a pan over a medium heat. Add the celery and carrot and sauté for 3–4 minutes until softened, then add the beef mince and cook for 3–4 minutes until browned.
3. Deglaze the pan with the white wine, and when the alcohol has cooked off, add the marinated onions and bay leaves. Simmer over a low heat for about 15 minutes, before tasting and seasoning with salt and freshly ground black pepper. Remove the bay leaves.
4. In the meantime, bring a pot of generously salted water to the boil. Cook the pasta until al dente, following the packet instructions. Once the pasta is al dente, drain and add to the pan with the ragù, tossing to combine.
5. Plate and serve immediately with freshly grated Parmesan to taste.

Orecchiette with aubergine pesto

ORECCHIETTE AL PESTO DI MELANZANE

serves 6

We are obliged to forewarn you that this pesto will win no beauty awards. Those who have prepared baba ganoush, a Middle Eastern mezze made in a similar way to this pesto, will testify that the flesh of roasted aubergines has a sort of cadaverous property, slimy and pallid-looking. Luckily, it tastes fantastic, particularly when it's allowed to blacken a little, taking on lots of smoky flavour. So do not be disheartened when preparing this *pesto di melanzane* if it looks less than inviting: the flavour of the end result will, we promise, redeem all its ugly sin.

2 aubergines, halved

150ml extra virgin olive oil, plus extra to drizzle

100g pistachios or blanched almonds, plus a few crushed nuts to serve

7–8 fresh basil leaves

70g Parmesan, or vegetarian alternative, grated

750g orecchiette

Sea salt flakes, to taste

1. Preheat the oven to 180°C. Place the aubergines on a baking tray, then sprinkle with sea salt flakes and drizzle with extra virgin olive oil. Bake for 20–25 minutes, or until soft.

2. Let the aubergine halves cool slightly before scooping out the pulp, removing any big clumps of seeds in the process.

3. Meanwhile, toast the pistachios or almonds in a dry frying pan until fragrant, taking care not to burn them.

4. Place the pulp of the aubergine in a food processor with the olive oil, basil, cheese and pistachios or almonds and blend until the mixture is creamy. Taste for seasoning, adding more salt as required.

5. Bring a pot of generously salted water to the boil. Cook the pasta until al dente, following the packet instructions. Once the pasta is al dente, drain and return to the pot with the pesto, tossing to combine.

6. Plate and serve immediately, topped with a dusting of pistachio or almond crumbs.

THE POETRY OF PASTA

AS MIDDAY APPROACHES IN SICILY and the sun beats down on the foothills of Mount Etna, a wagon with broad wheels bumps along the dusty road. Its precious cargo of vegetables and bottles of deep red wine sway with the motion of the road. The wagon's driver sips from a flagon of water, mopping his brow. His journey is only partly complete, but he's famished after an early start and pulls into a local taverna for lunch. He's a man of simple tastes but a large appetite, and he orders a generous plate of *spaghetti alla carrettiera* (sometimes referred to as 'wanderer's' or 'wagoner's pasta') – olive oil flavoured with garlic, capers, sun-dried tomatoes and parsley, with a shower of crunchy, toasted breadcrumbs on top. It is peasant food of the most delicious and satisfying kind.

You see, it isn't just the pasta shapes in Italy that have wonderfully storied names. The titles of myriad sauces and ragùs serve to not only highlight their star ingredients (*crema al Gorgonzola*; *aglio, olio e peperoncino*; *salsa di asparagi*) or regions of origin (Bolognese, Amatriciana, Genovese), they sometimes hint of hidden depths and spicy backstories. *Arrabbiata*, for example, means 'angry' – an evocative name for a fiery red sauce flavoured heavily with garlic and fresh red chilli. And the Sicilian *carrettiere* is not the only tradesman with a signature dish named after him. *Pasta alla boscaiola*, 'woodsman's pasta', takes its name from the forests of Italy where mushrooms sprout abundantly. Spicy cured sausage also belongs here, with the dish whipped up in Tuscan kitchens after a long day of lumberjacking.

Pasta alla boscaiola, 'woodsman's pasta', takes its name from the forests of Italy where mushrooms sprout abundantly.

The true origin of the ubiquitous *pasta alla carbonara*, meanwhile, has long been disputed, although the dish itself was likely the result of a surfeit of eggs and bacon brought to Rome by American troops following the Second World War. The name, however, derived from *carbonaro*, or 'charcoal burner', married with the simple smoky flavour of the velvety sauce studded with pancetta, lends the dish a certain working man's mystique. Down the mines during the day, taking comfort in *carbonara* when arriving home in the evening.

Unsurprisingly perhaps, the impact of the American presence in Italy in the 1940s and 50s wasn't limited to such family-friendly dishes. *Pasta alla puttanesca*, the tomato sauce made punchy with capers, olives, anchovies and chillies, was born around the same time. *Puttana* translates to 'lady of the night'. In those difficult days after the war, and especially in Naples where this dish originates, some of the women of Italy were forced to make ends meet however they could. Quite how this pasta sauce came into it remains a mystery – some say it was a quick snack whipped up by those ladies between clients, others (with a twinkle in their eye) say it has something to do with the powerful and spicy aromas in the dish. In any event, the word is almost onomatopoeic – you can just imagine a working girl, short skirt, thick make-up, hint of garlic on her breath, posing in the light of a street lamp in Naples, full of sarcasm and sass, whispering a salty come hither . . .

Puttana translates to 'lady of the night'.

Orecchiette with beans & mussels

ORECCHIETTE CON FAGIOLI E COZZE *serves 4*

La cucina povera, best understood in English as 'the poor man's kitchen', is an approach to cooking from the Italian south. It emphasises the use of simple, affordable ingredients, and became established in the eighteenth and nineteenth centuries, when the south of Italy largely remained agrarian and impoverished. The industrialising northern metropolises, Milan or Turin for example, were all but unrecognisable to the southern citizens of the new Italian Republic, born only in 1861. Driven by destitution, millions of Italians from the south emigrated in search of a better life in the United States.

To this day in Italy, a gulf exists between north and south, not merely in economic terms but also along religious and cultural lines. The division is most striking in gastronomy, with pronounced regional preferences. Few Italians from the north, for example, could say they grew up on *pasta e fagioli*, or pasta and beans. This simple recipe remains a staple of the Italian south, and this version from Naples, with mussels, is a variation, but is scarcely more opulent: mussels, *cozze* in Italian, are among the most affordable seafood available.

6 tbsp extra virgin olive oil
1 garlic clove
1 fresh red chilli, cut in half
1 brown or white onion, chopped
1 celery stick, chopped
1 carrot, chopped
80–100g cherry tomatoes
500g mussels, rinsed and de-bearded
460g tinned white beans, drained
750g orecchiette
15–20g fresh parsley, chopped

1. Place 2 tablespoons of oil in a large frying pan over a medium heat. Once hot, add the garlic and the chilli and fry for a couple of minutes until golden and fragrant. Remove the garlic and chilli from the pan and discard.

2. Add the onion, celery and carrot to the pan and fry until softened, around 10 minutes. Add the tomatoes, then cover the pan with a lid and cook for a further 5 minutes.

3. In a separate pot over a medium heat, pour in the mussels with 100ml of water (around half a cup). As soon as the mussels start to open, remove them from the steaming liquid and set aside. Discard any that haven't opened. Strain the flavoursome cooking liquid through a tea strainer or muslin cloth and set aside.

4. Add the beans and mussels to the vegetables with the strained cooking liquid, and simmer for 4–5 minutes over a low heat.

5. While the sauce is cooking, bring a pot of generously salted water to the boil. Cook the pasta until al dente, following the packet instructions.

6. Once the pasta is al dente, drain and add to the sauce, then continue to cook for an additional 2 minutes. Add the parsley and remaining olive oil and serve immediately.

Baked rigatoni from Messina

RIGATONI 'NCASCIATA ALLA MESSINESE

serves 6

Imagine for a moment that you are around the table of a large Sicilian family. It's Sunday lunchtime, and all the relatives have gathered for the occasion. After much noisy catching up, the donna della casa emerges from the kitchen with a piping hot tray of *pasta 'ncasciata*, heralding the happy beginning of the family feast.

On the island, *pasta 'ncasciata* is something of a generic term. In the Sicilian language, *'ncasciata* simply means 'encased', in reference to the way this pasta is heartily contained within one sprawling tray for the whole family to feast upon. In this sense, there are almost countless variations of *pasta 'ncasciata*. In this version, from the city of Messina in the island's northeast, you'll find all manner of delicious things, but we most love the rustic, homely inclusion of boiled eggs. We like to use eggs with lovely golden yolks, as these seem to resemble the warm sunshine of Sicily overhead.

2 tbsp extra virgin olive oil
1 brown or white onion, diced
300g pork mince
300g beef mince
600g tomato passata
2 tsp sea salt flakes
150ml vegetable oil
2 aubergines, sliced lengthways
750g rigatoni
200g provolone or mozzarella, diced
120g 'nduja or sopressata sausage
4 eggs, hard-boiled, peeled and
    quartered (optional)
Pecorino Romano, grated, to taste

1. Preheat the oven to 200°C.
2. Heat the olive oil in a large saucepan over a gentle heat and fry the onion for 4 minutes until softened.
3. Increase the heat and add the pork and beef mince and brown evenly, stirring and scraping the bottom of the pan. After 3–4 minutes, once browned, add the passata and sea salt flakes, cover with a lid and simmer for 10 minutes over a low heat, stirring occasionally.
4. While the meat sauce simmers, add the vegetable oil to a separate frying pan and place over a medium-high heat. Once hot, fry the aubergines until golden brown, then remove from the pan and transfer to kitchen paper to absorb any excess oil.
5. Bring a pot of generously salted water to the boil. Cook the pasta until al dente, following the packet instructions. Once the pasta is al dente, drain and place in a bowl, tossing through a couple of spoonfuls of the ragù.

Spaghetti from Nerano

SPAGHETTI ALLA NERANO   *serves 4*

We love this recipe because of its ability to transport you to Italy. Specifically, the sun-drenched Sorrento peninsula, where this dish was invented in a beach village, Nerano, as recently as the 1950s. There's something emphatically Campanian about it: the provolone cheese, which is the star of the dish, originates near Mount Vesuvius, less than 50 kilometres away across the Bay of Naples. Nowadays, it's produced throughout Campania, and provolone del Monaco, made on the Sorrento peninsula, is preferred by locals in this recipe (but any provolone will be fantastic).

Courgettes, meanwhile, herald the arrival of summer in Campania; it's when they're in season and markets abound with them in all shapes and colours. These are most beautiful when they produce their orange-coloured blossoms. On occasion, these are also added to this sauce and look supremely pretty. And while it isn't necessarily traditional, Finn likes lemon zest in the sauce: it complements the courgettes so very well and somehow adds even more sunshine to the dish. This addition, though, is entirely discretionary.

6 tbsp extra virgin olive oil
*700g courgettes, peeled and sliced
    into 2cm coins*
500g spaghetti
1 garlic clove, peeled
200g provolone, grated
1 tbsp unsalted butter
*15–20g fresh basil leaves,
    roughly torn*
*Grated zest of 1 unwaxed lemon
    (optional)*
Salt and black pepper, to taste

1. Place the oil in a frying pan over a medium-high heat. Fry the courgette slices in batches, removing the slices when they soften and transferring them to kitchen paper to absorb the excess oil. Continue this process until all the courgettes have been fried. Take the pan off the heat but leave the remaining oil in the pan.

2. Bring a pot of generously salted water to the boil. Cook the pasta until al dente, following the packet instructions. While the pasta cooks, prepare the sauce.

3. Return the frying pan with oil to the heat and add the garlic clove. Gently brown the garlic clove for 2 minutes until the oil is fragrant. Remove the garlic from the pan and discard.

4. Return the courgettes to the pan with the oil, sautéing for a minute or two over a medium heat. Drain the spaghetti, reserving a splash of the starchy pasta cooking water, and add the spaghetti to the courgettes.

5. Remove the pan from the heat, then add the provolone, butter, basil and lemon zest, if using. Stir the mixture until well combined, adding as much of the reserved cooking water as necessary to obtain a creamy sauce. Season with salt and black pepper to taste and serve immediately.

Rigatoni with Sicily's aubergine sauce

RIGATONI ALLA NORMA

V/Ve

serves 4

On the sun-drenched island of Sicily, aubergines are widely grown, both commercially and in islanders' gardens. Though *melanzane*, as Italians call aubergines, are enjoyed throughout Italy, they've particularly ensconced themselves in the gastronomic heart of Sicily. *Pasta alla norma* hails from the island's second city, Catania. It is said that the dish is named after Norma, the opera by Vincenzo Bellini, in reference to its comparable degree of beauty. Ricotta salata is worth seeking out, not merely because it's the traditional accompaniment, but because it works so very well. It bears no resemblance to regular soft ricotta, so don't be tempted to substitute this; chunks of pecorino Romano, or crumbled feta, would be better alternatives.

2 large aubergines
3 tsp sea salt flakes
650g tinned tomatoes,
*   peeled (ideally the San*
*   Marzano variety)*
3 tbsp extra virgin olive oil
1 garlic clove, peeled
15–20g fresh basil leaves, finely
*   shredded*
300ml vegetable oil
500g rigatoni
Salt and black pepper, to taste
Ricotta salata, to serve

1. Cut the aubergine into 1cm thick slices, place in a bowl and sprinkle over 2 teaspoons of sea salt flakes. This will draw out any excess moisture from the aubergines.

2. Heat the olive oil in a large saucepan over a medium heat and add the garlic clove. Fry for a few minutes, until the oil is fragrant and infused with the garlic flavour. Remove the garlic from the pan and discard.

3. Add the tomatoes to the pan with a few basil leaves and the remaining sea salt flakes. Cook for around 15 minutes, lightly crushing the tomatoes as they soften to form a rough sauce.

4. Drain the aubergine and pat dry with kitchen paper. In a separate frying pan, heat the vegetable oil and fry the aubergine in batches. Once softened, remove the aubergine from the pan and place on more kitchen paper to absorb any excess oil.

5. Set aside four slices of the fried aubergine as a garnish. Cut the remaining slices into rough chunks before adding to the tomato sauce. Reduce the heat and let the sauce simmer.

6. Bring a pot of generously salted water to the boil. Cook the pasta until al dente, following the packet instructions.

7. Once the pasta is al dente, reserve a splash of starchy pasta cooking water, then drain the pasta and add it to the sauce. Toss until completely coated, adding a little of the reserved cooking water to loosen the sauce, if needed.

8. Plate and serve immediately, garnished with the slices of aubergine and some crumbled ricotta salata.

Orecchiette with cime di rapa

ORECCHIETTE ALLE CIME DI RAPA

serves 4

This is one of Roberta's best-loved recipes. Orecchiette is, of course, her favourite pasta shape: the stuff she grew up on, and learned to make by hand from her nonna Maria-Assunta. Cime di rapa was equally focal in her upbringing. This green vegetable is eaten in several parts of Italy, notably in Naples, where it is known as *friarielli* and served on pizza with morsels of sausage. It has a bitter, pungent flavour that you may love or loathe. This recipe is with anchovies and overleaf with Italian sausage. You pick.

WITH ANCHOVIES

800g cime di rapa (or tenderstem broccoli, as an alternative)
4 tbsp extra virgin olive oil
100g breadcrumbs
1 garlic clove, minced
3–4 anchovies in oil
500g orecchiette
1 fresh red chilli, finely chopped (optional)
Salt, to taste

1. Prepare your cime di rapa by removing and discarding the hard stalks of the vegetable, reserving only the tender flowers and leaves. Rinse these well under running water.
2. Bring a pot of salted water to the boil and cook the cime di rapa for 10–15 minutes until soft and tender. Spear a piece with a fork to check if it's ready. Using a slotted spoon, remove the cime di rapa from the pot. Do not discard the cooking water.
3. Heat 1 tablespoon of oil in a frying pan over a medium heat. Add the breadcrumbs and toast for a few minutes, stirring to ensure even browning. Set to one side. Wipe the pan dry.
4. Add the remaining oil to the pan, then fry the garlic gently for 2 minutes until fragrant. Add the anchovies, allowing them to melt and separate in the hot oil. Remove any larger bones if necessary. Add the cime di rapa to the garlic and anchovy mixture.
5. Bring the pot with the cooking water back to the boil, then add the pasta and cook until very al dente, removing from the heat 2 minutes or so before the packet instructions say.
6. While the pasta cooks, take a spoonful or two of the starchy pasta cooking water and add this to the cime di rapa mixture. Cook the mixture on high, stirring regularly until a glossy sauce is formed.
7. Drain the pasta and add to the pan containing the cime di rapa. Stir to combine and continue to cook for a further 5 minutes.
8. Taste and season with salt and fresh chilli. Serve immediately, garnished with a scattering of toasted breadcrumbs.

WITH SAUSAGE

850g cime di rapa (or tenderstem
    broccoli, as an alternative)
8 tbsp extra virgin olive oil
2 garlic cloves, peeled and
    lightly crushed
1 whole dried red chilli
450g Italian sausage meat
    (ideally infused with fennel),
    crumbled
100ml dry white wine
500g orecchiette
Salt, to taste
Parmesan, or vegetarian alternative,
    grated, to serve

1. Prepare your cime di rapa by removing and discarding the hard
   stalks of the vegetable, reserving only the tender flowers and
   leaves. Rinse these well under running water.
2. Bring a pot of salted water to the boil and cook the cime di rapa
   in the water for around 10–15 minutes, until soft and tender.
   Spear a piece with a fork to check if it's ready. Strain and set
   aside to cool. Once cooled, roughly chop.
3. Place the oil in a large frying pan over a medium heat. Once hot,
   add the garlic cloves and the dried chilli and fry for a couple of
   minutes until the oil is well infused. Remove the garlic and chilli
   from the pan and discard.
4. Add the sausage meat to the pan, using a fork or wooden spatula
   to break the meat into small pieces, and fry for 2 minutes until
   nicely browned. Add the white wine and allow the alcohol to
   cook off before adding the chopped cime di rapa, then sauté the
   mixture for a couple of minutes.
5. Bring a pot of generously salted water to the boil. Cook the pasta
   until al dente, following the packet instructions.
6. Once the pasta is al dente, reserve a cup of the starchy pasta
   cooking water, then drain the pasta. Add the pasta to the sausage
   mixture, tossing until well combined, and adding a drop of the
   cooking water to loosen the sauce, if needed.
7. Plate and serve immediately with freshly grated Parmesan to
   taste.

Orecchiette with rocket and potatoes

ORECCHIETTE CON RUCOLA E PATATE

serves 6

This was the favourite dish of Roberta's late nonna, Maria-Assunta, and its inclusion in this book is a tribute to her. Wild rocket grows spontaneously across Puglia. Familiar with the land through years of working it, Maria-Assunta knew the best places to find rocket growing. As a young girl, Roberta joined her in search of the herb in the early mornings before the sun became too hot. The duo would return to the farmhouse only once they had amassed a sprawling basketful, which would then be used to prepare the dish we're making here in honour of the d'Elia family.

An emblem of poor cuisine in the north of Puglia, the rocket provides a natural spiciness and flavour, while potatoes are historically the nutritional mainstay of peasant cuisine here. Roberta adores this recipe precisely because it is simple. It has no pretensions. This was – remains – a peasant's dish. For Roberta, though, it just tastes of home.

4 tbsp extra virgin olive oil
1 garlic clove, minced
450g fresh tomatoes, peeled
*   and diced*
4 medium-sized potatoes,
*   peeled and diced*
300g rocket
750g orecchiette
1 fresh red chilli, seeds removed
*   and finely chopped*
Salt and black pepper, to taste

1. Heat the oil in a large saucepan over a medium heat and fry the garlic for a minute or two until fragrant and golden, taking care not to burn it.
2. Add the tomatoes to the pan and cook over a medium heat for 20 minutes.
3. While the tomato sauce is cooking, bring a large pot of generously salted water to the boil. Submerge the chunks of potato in the water for around 10 minutes until softened. Then add the rocket and pasta, cooking for as long as the pasta packet instructs.
4. When ready, drain the pasta, potato and rocket before returning to the pot. Pour over the tomato sauce, add the red chilli and toss together to combine. Plate and serve immediately.

Make your own
ZUPPA DI PASTA

Zuppa di pasta, simply 'pasta soup', is a staple across Italy. Like many peasant foods, it's somehow ensconced itself in the country's culinary tradition and now conjures up cosy feelings of warmth and comfort. This is particularly so during winter, when Italians across the country take great joy in preparing a pasta soup with scarcely any ingredients. We've brought you three of our favourite regional variations here. We hope they will sustain and warm you through the cold winter nights, as they have done us on countless occasions.

BASE RECIPE (SERVES 4)

- Heat 3 tbsp olive oil in a pan over a medium-high heat.
- Add 50g finely chopped white or brown onion and 50g finely shredded carrot and cook for 3–4 minutes until softened.
- Add the next batch of ingredients, as specified in the various regional options.

Piedmont

Zuppa di ceci (chickpea pasta soup). Add **300g cooked chickpeas** and allow them to brown for a few minutes. Cover with **200ml hot vegetable stock** and add **60g tomato purée**, **2 bay leaves** and **a sprig of rosemary**. Give the soup a good stir, season to taste and cook for 5 minutes or so. Then add **500g dried pasta** and cook until al dente, following packet instructions.

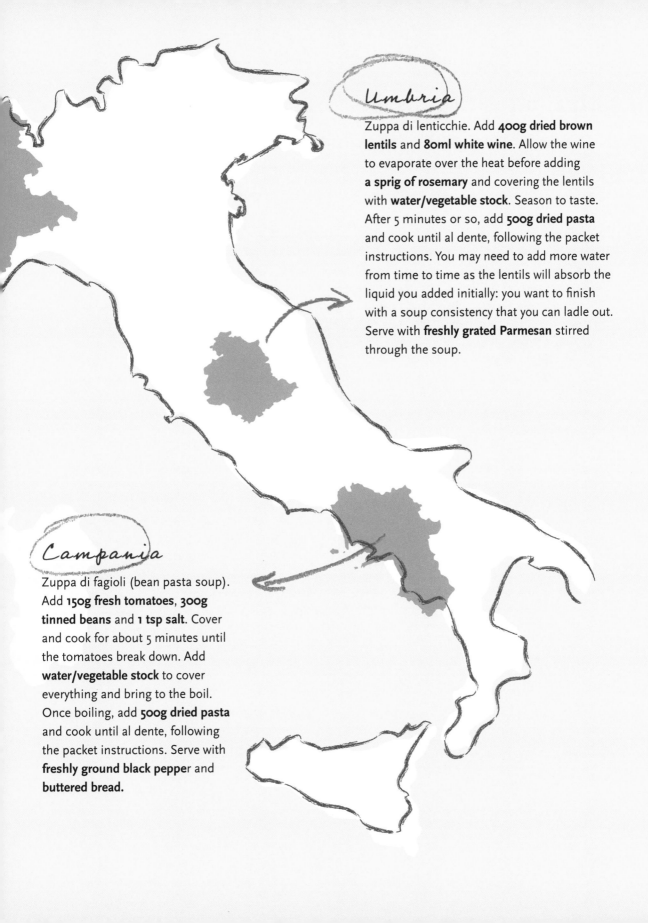

Umbria

Zuppa di lenticchie. Add **400g dried brown lentils** and **80ml white wine**. Allow the wine to evaporate over the heat before adding **a sprig of rosemary** and covering the lentils with **water/vegetable stock**. Season to taste. After 5 minutes or so, add **500g dried pasta** and cook until al dente, following the packet instructions. You may need to add more water from time to time as the lentils will absorb the liquid you added initially: you want to finish with a soup consistency that you can ladle out. Serve with **freshly grated Parmesan** stirred through the soup.

Campania

Zuppa di fagioli (bean pasta soup). Add **150g fresh tomatoes, 300g tinned beans** and **1 tsp salt**. Cover and cook for about 5 minutes until the tomatoes break down. Add **water/vegetable stock** to cover everything and bring to the boil. Once boiling, add **500g dried pasta** and cook until al dente, following the packet instructions. Serve with **freshly ground black pepper** and **buttered bread.**

Rigatoni with sausage & saffron

RIGATONI ALLA MONZESE

serves 6

In northern Lombardy, modestly south of Lake Como and the Alps, you'll find a historical region called Brianza. It's an idyllic place, hilly and green with lakes that have offered escapism to the people of nearby Milan for centuries. Its fertile land has also supported all manner of agriculture for generations, but pigs, reared extensively in the region, are central to the story of Brianza.

In Monza – the largest settlement of Brianza – pig farming has given rise to a strong predilection for sausage. The speciality sausage of the city, *la luganega di Monza*, includes several distinctive ingredients, from Grana Padano cheese to Marsala wine, imbuing the sausage with a wonderful, unusual flavour. Monza's eponymous *pasta alla Monzese* celebrates these flavours, allowing them to infuse the cream, with silky strands of saffron, added during cooking, giving a golden lustre. While *luganega di Monza* is almost impossible to find outside of Lombardy, let alone here in the UK, any good sausage meat with a high pork content will work wonderfully. Children happen to love this recipe too, so you can serve it with confidence whatever the occasion.

350g Italian sausage meat (ideally infused with fennel), crumbled

200ml double cream

15g saffron

750g rigatoni

Salt and black pepper, to taste

Parmesan, grated, to serve

1. Fry the sausage meat in a pan over a medium-high heat for 4–5 minutes until cooked, using a fork or wooden spatula to break the meat into small pieces.

2. Turn the heat down and add the cream and saffron. Continue cooking for 5–7 minutes, then season with salt and black pepper to taste.

3. Bring a pot of generously salted water to the boil. Cook the pasta until al dente, following the packet instructions. Once the pasta is al dente, drain and add to the sauce, tossing to combine.

4. Plate and serve immediately with freshly grated Parmesan to taste.

Malloreddus with lentil ragù

MALLOREDDUS AL RAGÙ DI LENTICCHIE

V/Ve

serves 4

The Greek philosopher Diogenes, seen taking a modest meal of lentils, was mocked by his sycophant peer Aristippus: 'You needn't live on lentils if you would only learn to flatter the king.' Diogenes, with a twinkle in his eye (or so we imagine), responded, 'If you would only learn to live on lentils you needn't flatter the king.' Although Diogenes lived some three centuries before the days of Ancient Rome, his understanding of the humble lentil – as a sort of edible emancipation, freeing the poor from supplication to higher powers – was to prove prophetic.

Indeed, on the Italian peninsula, and particularly during the days of Rome, lentils, or *lenticchie* in Italian, have sustained peasants for millennia. They are now synonymous with good fortune and health in modern Italy. In fact, lentils are traditionally enjoyed on New Year's Eve alongside *cotechino* sausage; the lentils, reminiscent of little coins in shape, are said to augur well for the year ahead.

We like to cook and eat lentils year-round, and not merely as a substitute or stand-in for meat, as they are often prescribed. In many ways, this simple, homely ragù shows that they can be an altogether more satisfying ingredient.

6–7 tbsp extra virgin olive oil
1 celery stick, finely chopped
1 carrot, finely chopped
1 garlic clove, minced
1 brown or white onion, finely chopped
1 fresh red chilli, seeds removed and finely chopped
600g dried puy lentils, rinsed
70g cherry tomatoes, halved
Sprig of fresh thyme
750g malloreddus
Salt and black pepper, to taste
Parmesan, or vegetarian alternative, grated, to serve

1. Heat 2 tablespoons of oil in a saucepan and sweat the celery, carrot, garlic and onion for 3–4 minutes over a medium heat until soft and translucent. Add the finely chopped chilli and cook for a further minute or so.

2. Add the lentils, stirring well, then add the cherry tomatoes with a pinch of salt and pepper. Add enough water to cover the mixture and simmer over a low heat until the lentils are soft (around 10–12 minutes).

3. Stir often, adding more water if necessary. Once the lentils are soft and have absorbed the water, season again with salt and pepper, then add the thyme leaves (leave out the sprig itself) and a drizzle of olive oil.

4. While the sauce is cooking, bring a pot of generously salted water to the boil. Cook the pasta until al dente, following the packet instructions. Once the pasta is al dente, drain and add to the sauce, tossing to combine.

5. Plate and serve immediately with freshly grated Parmesan and a drizzle of olive oil to taste.

Pappardelle with cod & cherry tomatoes

PAPPARDELLE AL SUGO DI MERLUZZO E POMODORINO   *serves 6*

When Finn was last in Parma, he found himself bemused reading a restaurant menu. While every other word was in Italian, the very English 'cod' stuck out like a sore thumb. Alessandro, who was joining him for dinner, explained that the Italian word for cod, *merluzzo*, has a second-rate ring to it. And so, where the fish is served, and particularly in fancy restaurants, the English translation is preferred by proprietors, as though they are disguising something wholly unwelcome.

In any case, pasta with fillets of fresh cod is enjoyed widely throughout Italy, and almost always served with very sweet and diminutive cherry tomatoes. While Roberta might feel slightly abashed to serve up merluzzo, Finn has no such qualms, and finds this a satisfying supper best enjoyed in the evening sunshine.

6 tbsp extra virgin olive oil

1 garlic clove, peeled and lightly crushed

1 fresh red chilli, cut in half (optional)

400g cod fillets, cleaned and roughly diced

100ml white wine

120g cherry tomatoes, diced

15g fresh basil leaves, roughly torn

750g pappardelle

Salt and black pepper, to taste

15g fresh parsley, finely chopped, to serve

1. Place the oil in a large frying pan over a low heat. Once hot, add the garlic and the chilli, if using, and fry for a couple of minutes until golden and fragrant. Remove the garlic and chilli from the pan and discard.
2. Increase the heat and add the cod. Let it brown slightly for a couple of minutes, stirring often, then slowly pour in the white wine and let it evaporate.
3. Add the tomatoes and basil, stir gently and season with salt and pepper. Cook for 8–10 minutes over a moderate heat.
4. Meanwhile, bring a pot of generously salted water to the boil. Cook the pasta until al dente, following the packet instructions.
5. Once the pasta is al dente, reserve a cup of the starchy pasta cooking water, then drain the pasta and add to the sauce. Stir gently over a low heat for 2 minutes, adding some of the reserved cooking water to loosen the sauce, if needed.
6. Plate and serve immediately, topped with the parsley.

Malloreddus with sausage ragù from Sardinia

serves 4

MALLOREDDUS ALLA CAMPIDANESE

In Sardinia, an Italian island of the Mediterranean, you can ask any passerby – albeit in Sardu, the local language – what the secret to the island's special ragù is. They will tell you that the perfect *ragù alla Campidanese* (named after the island's Campidano region) relies on the use of as few ingredients as possible. Each, however, should be of the highest quality you can find. We should mention, too, that fennel seeds are central to this recipe. If you consider yourself a detractor – and many do when it comes to fennel – we urge you: take a leap of faith and indulge us. You will be glad you did.

2 tbsp extra virgin olive oil

1 brown or white onion, finely diced

400g Italian sausage meat (ideally infused with fennel), crumbled

400g tomato passata

1 tbsp fennel seeds

500g malloreddus

Salt and black pepper, to taste

Parmesan, pecorino Romano, or vegetarian alternative, grated, to serve

1. Heat the olive oil in a frying pan over a medium-high heat. Add the onion and fry for 4 minutes until soft and translucent.

2. Increase the heat slightly and add the sausage meat. Brown the sausage meat in the pan for 7–8 minutes, using a fork or wooden spatula to break the meat into small pieces. Once browned, return the heat to medium and add the passata, fennel seeds, salt and black pepper. Simmer until the sausage is fully cooked and the mixture has thickened – this will take around 15 minutes.

3. While the sauce cooks, bring a pot of generously salted water to the boil. Cook the pasta until al dente, following the packet instructions.

4. Once the pasta is al dente, reserve a cup of the starchy pasta cooking water, then drain the pasta. Add the pasta to the sauce, tossing until it's completely coated, adding a drop of the cooking water to loosen the sauce, if needed.

5. Plate and serve immediately with freshly grated Parmesan or pecorino Romano to taste.

Spaghetti frittata

FRITTATA DI SPAGHETTI AL FORNO   *serves 4*

Most Italians, and especially Roberta, baulk at the idea of food waste. When an excess of leftovers does mount up, though, the *frittata di pasta* offers recourse. Reminiscent of Britain's bubble and squeak, made from the inevitable leftovers of roast dinners, Roberta's version is inspired by Neapolitan tradition. In Naples, it's common for the spaghetti frittata to be referred to as a *pastiera di spaghetti*, in reference to the city's similar-looking *pastiera* tart.

In any case, the dish is largely a product of whichever ingredients you have to hand. In Roberta's kitchen, there's almost always smoked scamorza cheese, as well as guanciale or pancetta, so these come heartily recommended. Ultimately, though, you can use whatever you have to accompany the leftover pasta and eggs. There is no reason this frittata must be assembled with spaghetti, either; any leftover pasta shape will work just as well. To Roberta's horror, Finn quite likes to have a slice for breakfast, dunked in full-fat mayonnaise with sea salt flakes sprinkled over.

8 medium eggs

15g fresh parsley, finely chopped

40g Parmesan, grated

100g smoked scamorza, cubed

20ml whole milk

1 tsp sea salt flakes

Freshly ground black pepper, to taste

500g cooked spaghetti

4 tbsp extra virgin olive oil

120g pancetta or guanciale, cubed

1. Crack the eggs into a large bowl. Beat them lightly, then add the chopped parsley, Parmesan, smoked scamorza, milk, salt and pepper. Add the spaghetti and stir gently until well combined.
2. Heat the oil in a large non-stick frying pan over a medium heat. Add the pancetta or guanciale and fry until crisp (around 4 minutes). Then, add the egg and spaghetti mixture and spread evenly over the pan. Cover with a lid and cook for 10 minutes over a medium-low heat.
3. Using the pan's lid for support, flip the frittata and return to the frying pan in order to cook the other side. Fry for another 5 minutes or so. Alternatively, if your pan can go under the grill, this will also work to set the frittata without the need to flip it.
4. With a sharp knife, cut the frittata into four and serve immediately.

PART 4

SPECIAL RECIPES

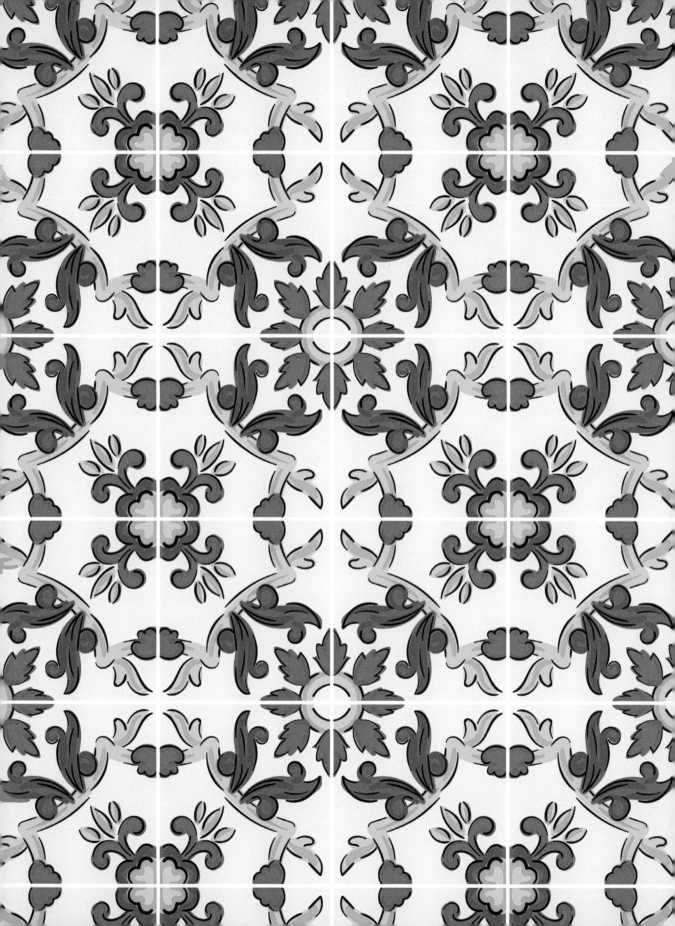

In the modern age, many of us lead increasingly complicated and frenetic lives. There's much talk of populations becoming 'time poor', whether through longer working hours, the need to commute to our offices, or simply from spending more time on our myriad devices and social media. In some respects, the 'time poverty' phenomenon has served us well at Pasta Evangelists, as the dishes we deliver to our customers, comprising freshly made pasta and sauces, require only five minutes or so of preparation on the customer's part.

On the other hand, we regret that people's lives are busier than ever, as some of our favourite and most-treasured recipes are those that are made over the course of several hours. 'Time poverty' is also the antithesis of traditional Italian life, which many of us at Pasta Evangelists look to with fondness and admiration. If you visit the island of Sardinia, for example, which is home to some of the oldest and healthiest people on our planet, locals will emphasise the need to live slowly and with as little stress as possible. They sow their own seeds, harvest their own vegetables and take great relish in a glass of local wine at lunchtime. They do not lead sedentary lives, but nor do they sprint through their days, preferring to savour the moments human life bestows. For Sardinians, three moments lived well each day are better than thirty lived briskly. For a whole host of reasons (and perhaps most importantly because Roberta and Finn both have an aversion to sprinting that goes back to their schooldays), this approach to life strikes us as the right one.

Of course, life is also what it is. For all our wishing, we cannot just click our fingers and spread Sardinian languor throughout London, where we live. In many ways, we don't want to either. We love the city, with its eccentricity, opportunities and diversity (especially of its restaurants). We do think it's important, though, from time to time, to take a weekend to ourselves without any plans. When we do so, and can relax fully in the knowledge that there are no other obligations to fulfil, it's these special recipes that we love to cook. It should be said, too, that they are not special because they're taxing, or require strange and esoteric ingredients that you'd be hard-pressed to find in Italy, let alone outside of the country. They're special because, in a world where time can seem so hard to come by, it's this ingredient, perhaps the rarest of all, that brings these recipes so deliciously to life.

Tagliatelle with Bolognese sauce

TAGLIATELLE ALLA BOLOGNESE

serves 4

'Spaghetti Bolognese', as Italians see it, is the greatest affront perpetrated on their nation by the Anglo-Saxon world. Forget the collapse of the Roman Empire and Britannia's great revolt – far more traumatising, in the Italian perspective, is the proliferation of the pseudo-Italian spaghetti Bolognese throughout the world. We say 'pseudo' because – to be clear – there is nothing Italian about spaghetti Bolognese. And though you might even have been served the dish in Italy, perhaps while holidaying in Rome, Italians will insist you ate in a tourist trap, one where both chef and proprietor weep with shame at the end of each day, having sold their souls down the Tiber.

With emotions running high, we believe in doing what we can to salve Italy's wounded culinary consciousness. That's why, as the real Bolognese recipe calls for, we serve this sauce only with tagliatelle. Like the eponymous Bolognese sauce, tagliatelle comes from the city of Bologna, one of the world's great food capitals, and is the only respectable pasta pairing for it. Aside from being traditional, it's also the practical choice: spaghetti, far thinner than tagliatelle, do a comparatively poor job of sopping up the meaty sauce, and should be avoided, not merely for the sake of Italian pride.

2 tbsp extra virgin olive oil
50g unsalted butter
1 carrot, finely chopped
1 celery stick, finely chopped
1 brown or white onion,
  finely chopped
350g minced beef
100g unsmoked pancetta, cubed
150ml red wine
70g tomato paste
250ml beef stock
500g tomato passata
500g tagliatelle
Salt and black pepper, to taste
Parmesan, grated, to serve

1. Heat the olive oil and butter in a pan over a medium heat and fry the carrots, celery and onion for 4 minutes until lightly browned.
2. Add the minced beef and cook for 5–6 minutes until browned, stirring occasionally. Add the pancetta and cook for 3 minutes until crispy. Then deglaze the pan with a glass of red wine (150ml), cooking for 2 minutes until the alcohol evaporates.
3. Dissolve the tomato paste in half of the beef stock, then add to the pan and stir until well combined.
4. Add the passata, a splash of water and salt and pepper, mix well and simmer for about 2 hours, gradually adding the remaining broth as needed if it becomes too thick.
5. Bring a pot of generously salted water to the boil. Cook the pasta until al dente, following the packet instructions.
6. Once the pasta is al dente, reserve a small cup of the pasta cooking water, then drain the pasta and add to the sauce, tossing to combine. Add the cooking water as necessary to loosen the ragù.
7. Plate and serve immediately with a generous helping of grated Parmesan on top.

The ultimate lasagne

LASAGNA CLASSICA ITALIANA   *serves 4*

The classic Italian lasagne, drenched in béchamel and full of rich, meaty flavour, is surely one of Italy's most iconic dishes. Via the emigration of millions of destitute Italians in the nineteenth and twentieth centuries (particularly from Naples, where lasagne appears to have its origins), the dish was internationalised and propelled to global stardom. Nowhere is this truer than in the United States, which has a voracious collective appetite for lasagne. However, most recipes in that country call for ricotta in place of béchamel. And while we don't value tradition for tradition's sake, we do find this to be aberrant. A rich and creamy béchamel is, in our minds, just as integral to *lasagna classica Italiana* as its eponymous pasta sheets.

FOR THE BÉCHAMEL

60g unsalted butter
60g plain flour
600ml whole milk
½ tsp nutmeg, grated
Salt and black pepper, to taste

FOR THE LASAGNE

1 quantity Beef Shin Ragù
    (see page 203)
500g lasagne pasta sheets
75g Parmesan, grated,
    plus extra to serve

1. Make the béchamel. Melt the butter in a saucepan over a medium heat and add the flour, whisking until combined, then cook on a low heat for 1–2 minutes.
2. Reduce the heat to low and gradually add the milk, stirring continuously until the sauce is thickened. Season with nutmeg, salt and black pepper, and set aside.
3. Preheat the oven to 180°C.
4. To assemble the lasagne, ladle a thin layer of ragù over the bottom of a 25 x 19cm baking dish. Top with a layer of lasagne sheets – don't worry if they overlap a little. Follow this with another layer of ragù, using the back of the spoon to push it right to the edges. Follow with a layer of béchamel and sprinkle over a generous handful of grated Parmesan.
5. Repeat the following steps – pasta, ragù, béchamel, Parmesan – until both sauces and pasta are used up. Aim for around five layers of pasta, and don't forget to top with a generous amount of grated Parmesan.
6. Cook the lasagne for 40 minutes, covering with aluminium foil for the first 10–15 minutes to ensure it doesn't dry out in the oven or become too browned on top.
7. Remove from the oven and leave to stand for at least 5 minutes. To serve, slice into equal-sized portions and top with freshly grated Parmesan.

Make your own
LASAGNE

BASE RECIPE (SERVES 4)

FOR THE MEAT COMPONENT

- Choose your preferred additions from the regions opposite.
- Heat 3 tbsp olive oil in a pan over a medium-high heat.
- Add 50g finely chopped white or brown onion, 50g finely chopped celery and 50g finely diced carrot and cook for 3–4 minutes until softened.
- Add 750g beef mince in two batches and cook for 10 minutes or so until browned all over.
- Add 800g tomato passata and bring to the boil.
- Add salt and pepper to taste and allow to simmer for up to 30 minutes. Add a splash of water from time to time if the sauce becomes too thick.

FOR THE BÉCHAMEL COMPONENT

- Melt 100g unsalted butter in a saucepan. Once melted, stir in 100g plain white flour and cook gently for just under a minute.
- Gradually stir in 1 litre of whole milk, a little at a time, stirring well so that no lumps form. Bring the mixture to the boil, stirring constantly, so that the mixture thickens and becomes glossy.

CONSTRUCTING THE LASAGNE

- Ladle a thin layer of the meat sauce over the base of a medium to large baking dish.
- Top with a layer of lasagne sheets – don't worry if they overlap.
- Follow this with another layer of meat sauce, using the back of a spoon to push it right to the edges.
- Follow with a layer of béchamel.
- Repeat these steps until both sauces are used up.

Calabria

Add **small teaspoons of spicy 'nduja sausage**, about 100g in total, to each layer of the lasagne for a hot kick.

Sardinia

Substitute **lamb mince** for the **beef mince** in step 3 of the meat component.

Sicily

Fry **200g thinly sliced aubergines** in hot olive oil before drying off the excess oil. Add the fried aubergine alongside the mince when creating each layer of the lasagne.

'Breakfast in Tuscany' lasagne

'UN RISVEGLIO IN TOSCANA' LASAGNA

serves 6

Breakfast has always been Finn's favourite meal especially when, after a few too many the night before, he's feeling decidedly ropey. On one such morning, contending with a hangover at Pasta Evangelists' headquarters, he considered the merits of a full English breakfast. He sensed that rustling this up in the staff kitchen would betray his condition, so instead an office fridge raid yielding some leftover Tuscan sausage meat, pancetta and a couple of eggs provided the inspiration for this lasagne. Although traditional in absolutely no sense of the word, it is entirely delicious and the perfect salve for weary souls.

FOR THE LASAGNE

400g Italian sausage meat (ideally infused with fennel)
160g smoked pancetta, cubed
500g lasagne pasta sheets
75g Parmesan, grated, plus extra to serve
4–5 medium eggs

FOR THE BÉCHAMEL

40g unsalted butter
60g plain flour
600ml whole milk
½ tsp grated nutmeg
Salt and black pepper, to taste

1. For the lasagne, place a large pan over a medium heat and add the sausage meat, breaking it up with a wooden spoon. Continue to move the pieces in the pan to ensure they cook evenly and don't burn. After 4–6 minutes, once fully cooked, remove from the pan and set aside. Leave any rendered fat in the pan.

2. Add the pancetta to the pan and fry for 3–4 minutes until crisp. Once cooked, remove the pancetta and transfer the remaining fat to a clean saucepan.

3. To make the béchamel, heat the saucepan containing the fat over a medium heat and add the butter. Allow the butter to melt before adding the flour, whisking until combined, then cook on a low heat for 1–2 minutes, until a roux is formed.

4. Remove the pan from the heat and gradually add the milk, stirring continuously until thickened. Ensure you add only a splash of milk at a time. Season with nutmeg, salt and black pepper, and set aside. Preheat the oven to 180°C.

5. To assemble, ladle a thin layer of the béchamel sauce over the bottom of a 25cm x 19cm baking dish. Top with a layer of lasagne sheets – don't worry if they overlap a little. Follow this with a more generous layer of béchamel. Top this with a layer of the sausage and pancetta pieces, then sprinkle over some Parmesan.

6. Repeat the following steps – pasta, béchamel, meat, Parmesan – until all the sauce and pasta are used up. Aim for around five layers of pasta, and top generously with grated Parmesan.

7. Bake the lasagne for 30–35 minutes until crispy, covering with aluminium foil for the first 10–15 minutes to ensure it doesn't

dry out in the oven or become too browned on top. While the lasagne is baking, boil the eggs for 7 minutes. Allow to cool in cold water and then peel carefully.

8. Remove the lasagne from the oven. Using a knife, make 8–10 egg-shaped indentations in the top of your lasagne. Cut the peeled, soft-boiled eggs in half with a knife and insert an egg half in each of the indentations you have made, sunny side up. Cook for a further 2 minutes in the oven to finish.

9. Remove from the oven and leave to stand for at least 5 minutes. To serve, slice into equal-sized portions and top with freshly grated Parmesan. Happy breakfasting in Tuscany.

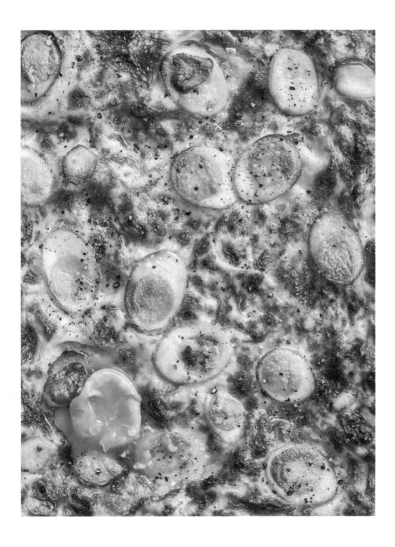

Pappardelle with beef shin ragù

PAPPARDELLE AL RAGÙ DI MANZO   *serves 4*

This was one of our very first dishes when we started Pasta Evangelists, and perhaps the one that has returned to our menu the most since then. It's an emphatic customer favourite, and one that we also eat on a weekly (if not daily, if we're being honest) basis.

What's so special about this dish is its apparent sumptuousness, with its bounty of melt-in-the-mouth meatiness. In reality, its preparation, involving the slow cooking of an otherwise tough cut, reminds us of the frugality of Tuscany's peasantry through the centuries. Although there's a scarce amount of preparation involved, you can't skimp on the slow cooking time here; the shin cut requires a good few hours to attain a rich, silky consistency, where the meat ceases to cling to the bone and yields all its wonderful flavours.

2 tbsp extra virgin olive oil

300g beef shin, cut into large chunks

2 garlic cloves, finely chopped

1 large brown or white onion, finely chopped

2 carrots, finely chopped

2 large celery sticks, finely chopped

3 tbsp tomato purée

500ml tomato passata

100ml good red wine (we like Barolo here)

200ml beef stock

1 bay leaf

500g pappardelle

Salt and black pepper, to taste

Parmesan, grated, to serve

1. Heat the oil in a large saucepan over a medium-high heat. Brown the beef shin on all sides, for about 5 minutes, working in batches if necessary. Once browned, set the beef aside.

2. Add the garlic and onion to the same pan and reduce the heat to medium. Sauté until fragrant and beginning to brown, around 2 minutes, then add the carrots and celery and continue to sauté until the vegetables are softened, about 5 minutes. Add the tomato purée along with the passata and cook for another few minutes.

3. Add the red wine and deglaze the pan, then simmer until reduced by half, about 5 minutes.

4. Once the wine has reduced, return the beef to the pan with the beef stock and bay leaf. Bring the liquid to a simmer over a medium-low heat, then cover and continue to simmer for 4 hours, or until the beef is very tender.

5. After 4 hours, remove the bay leaf. If the sauce is too thin, remove the beef and set aside. Continue reducing the liquid over a medium heat for a further 10 minutes until thickened. Pull the meat into shreds and stir through the sauce, then taste for seasoning, adding salt and pepper if necessary.

6. Bring a pot of generously salted water to the boil. Cook the pasta until al dente, following the packet instructions. Once the pasta is al dente, drain and add to the sauce, tossing to combine.

7. Plate and serve immediately, topped with grated Parmesan.

Pistachio & mortadella lasagne

LASAGNA AL PISTACCHIO E MORTADELLA *serves 6*

A combination of delicious things from both north and south, this is the embodiment of Italian unity: chaotic yet beautiful. Pistachios are the star of this dish. We love the way their jade hue gives the béchamel such a distinctive colour. Most of all, though, we love the texture and crunch they provide. But they aren't alone. Mortadella, a ham from the city of Bologna in the northern region of Emilia-Romagna, punctuates the lasagne's festive green with little studs of pink, and is just so pretty. The smoked mozzarella, a classic Neapolitan ingredient, adds further geographical diversity to the recipe and such incredible flavour.

If you are looking for a show-stopping dinner party dish, one that celebrates the very best of all Italy, this recipe is Roberta's favourite lasagne and comes with her strongest recommendation.

FOR THE BÉCHAMEL

100g unsalted butter
100g plain flour
1 litre whole milk
¾ tsp grated nutmeg
Salt and black pepper, to taste

FOR THE LASAGNE

300g Pistachio Pesto (see page 79)
500g lasagne pasta sheets
300g mortadella, diced into
    small pieces
350g smoked scamorza,
    diced into small pieces
80g Parmesan, grated
40g unsalted pistachio nuts,
    shelled and coarsely chopped

1. Begin by preparing the béchamel. Melt the butter in a saucepan over a low heat, then slowly add the flour, whisking until completely combined.
2. Heat the milk in a separate pan. Gradually add the heated milk to the butter and flour mixture over a low heat, stirring continuously to ensure no lumps form. Stir the sauce until thick enough to coat the back of a spoon, then add salt, pepper and grated nutmeg.
3. Combine the béchamel with the pistachio pesto to obtain a creamy sauce.
4. Preheat the oven to 200°C.
5. Spoon a couple of tablespoons of the pesto-béchamel mixture into the base of 25 x 19cm baking dish and spread to form an even layer. Cover with lasagne sheets – don't worry if they overlap a little. Then add another layer of the pesto-béchamel. Follow this with a scattering of the mortadella and smoked scamorza and top with some grated Parmesan.
6. Repeat the following steps – lasagne, pesto-béchamel, mortadella, mozzarella and Parmesan – until you have used up all the ingredients. You should have 4–5 layers of lasagne sheets.
7. Top with the chopped pistachios, cover with aluminium foil and bake for 40 minutes.
8. Once piping hot, remove from the oven and leave to cool for 5 minutes before serving.

Pappardelle with Tuscan wild boar ragù

PAPPARDELLE AL RAGÙ DI CINGHIALE

serves 6

In the city of Florence, you'll find *Il Porcelino* ('the piglet'), a statue by Baroque sculptor Pietro Tacca, dating back to the seventeenth century. Its name is misleading, for Tacca's masterpiece in bronze actually depicts an adult boar, complete with fearsome tusks. Although a regional mascot, boars are also a real nuisance. This brazen animal is often found gobbling grapes from growers' vines, snorting with delectation as it wreaks havoc. It's scarcely a surprise, then, that while you'll find the boar commemorated in statue form, you're just as likely to find it on the menu.

1kg wild boar meat (preferably shoulder), cut into 3cm cubes
750ml quality red wine
1 tbsp extra virgin olive oil
1 brown or white onion, finely chopped
1 carrot, finely chopped
1 celery stick, finely chopped
1 garlic clove, crushed
2 tbsp tomato purée
500ml chicken stock
3 bay leaves
3 sprigs of fresh thyme
10g juniper berries (if you can't find these, you can leave them out)
750g pappardelle
Salt and pepper, to taste
Parmesan, grated, to serve

1. Place the boar meat in a large mixing bowl and pour over the red wine. Cover and allow to marinate overnight or at least 4 hours.
2. Once the meat is ready, add the olive oil to a large pot over a medium heat. Add the onion, carrot and celery, and sweat the mixture for 4 minutes until soft and translucent. Add the garlic and continue to fry for 2 minutes more until fragrant.
3. Separate the cubes of boar from their red wine marinade and add the meat to the pot, setting aside the wine. Brown the meat, allowing it to fry for around 5 minutes.
4. Add the tomato purée and stir through, before deglazing the pan with half of the wine marinade. Once the alcohol has evaporated, add the chicken stock with the bay leaves, thyme and juniper berries. Stir until well mixed, then cover with a lid. Reduce the heat and allow to simmer and thicken for around 4 hours, stirring occasionally to avoid any sticking.
5. After 4 hours or so, check your ragù, it should be lighter in colour than when you left it. Check with a fork to see if the pieces of meat are falling apart. Once ready, turn off the heat, discard the thyme and bay leaves, and remove the meat from the pan, using two forks to tear it into tender shreds. Once shredded, return the meat to the pan. Leave on a very low simmer on the hob until it's ready to be served.
6. When it's time to serve, bring a pot of salted water to the boil. Cook the pasta until al dente, following the packet instructions.
7. Once the pasta is al dente, reserve a little of the starchy pasta cooking water, then drain the pasta and add to the sauce. Toss

together to coat, adding as much cooking water as necessary to ensure the pasta is well coated.

8. Plate and serve immediately with freshly grated Parmesan.

APERITIVO

IN ITALY, WHEN THE LATE AFTERNOON SUN begins to give way to evening's shadow, yet the air still feels warm and the mood languorous, it's usually time for *aperitivo*. This is far more than just a drink, as the French *apéritif* usually implies ('fancy an *apéritif*?'). Instead, the moment, the noun, *aperitivo* denotes a far richer moment. It's one of *convivialità*, a feeling of time spent together, and a prelude to the feast. One does not have 'an' *aperitivo*, either. Rather, one takes part 'in' *aperitivo*. This is because *aperitivo* is a sort of ritual, where stories are exchanged over finger foods and a good drink 'opens' an evening of eating (the Latin verb *aperire*, from which *aperitivo* derives, means 'to open').

It was this idea of 'opening' the meal that captured the imagination of the Torinese distiller Antonio Benedetto Carpano when he invented vermouth in the late eighteenth century. Aside from feeling that this aromatised wine was more 'befitting' for ladies than other local varieties, Carpano thought the herbs and spices used to infuse the wine, from cardamom and cinnamon to marjoram and chamomile, also had the desirable effect of stimulating the appetite. In this respect, his invention was posited as the drink of choice for a new tradition: *aperitivo*. The craze gripped Turin's high society, so much so that Carpano's wine shop was open around the clock. Cafés serving *stuzzichini* ('small bites') with vermouth soon popped up throughout Turin, widening access to a new *aperitivo* culture.

The Italian ritual of *aperitivo* has long since transcended the city of Turin, and is perhaps more closely associated with Milan today. However, although many think of *aperitivo* as something of a Milanese, or at least northern, tradition, the reality is that Italians from all four corners of the peninsula, and even its island extremities, merrily take part. In the southeastern region of Puglia, for example, Roberta recalls a particularly memorable *aperitivo* in the town of Gallipoli. There, *aperitivo* comes courtesy of the Ionian Sea and is often given the name *aperifish*, denoting morsels of fresh seafood taken with a cold beer and an ocean view. This take on *aperitivo* could scarcely be imagined in the heart of metropolitan Milan, but this makes it no less valid or meaningful.

Finn's favourite *aperitivo* comes from neither Turin nor Milan, but Venice, on the other side of northern Italy. It's the *spritz Veneziano*, ubiquitous in all its orange glory in the glasses of Venetians as they mingle along the city's canals, picking at little bites presented on wooden boards. For the uninitiated, the Venetian or Aperol spritz combines bitter Aperol with prosecco and soda. It's often served with a slice of fresh orange and plenty of ice, and is incredibly refreshing, particularly on a warm summer evening.

Other common sightings at *aperitivo* are the Campari spritz (the more astringent predecessor to the better-known Aperol version), as well as other bitter cocktails like Florence's Negroni and its ancestor, the Americano (whose name belies its Italian extraction). Countless other drinks can be found across Italy, like the increasingly popular Hugo spritz, originating in the Alpine region of South Tyrol. The most common drink during *aperitivo*, though, is probably a simple glass of dry white wine, produced locally and enjoyed similarly.

Ultimately, *aperitivo* is less about *what* one drinks and more about *how* one does so. No Italian, for example, could conceive of *aperitivo* without at least some food. This could be anything from a simple bowl of potato crisps through to a grandiose platter of cold cuts (usually it's somewhere inbetween), but *aperitivo* always means food. On this, all Italians can agree. So much so, in fact, that a new tradition, *apericena*, is establishing itself. Combining the word *aperitivo* with *cena* ('dinner'), it denotes an *aperitivo* so full of wonderful things to eat that there is no longer any need for a formal dinner in its wake. Equally, *aperitivo* is, by definition, a social occurrence: there is no such thing as *aperitivo* taken in solitude, and so *amici* and/or *famiglia* are invariably part of this special ritual wherever and whenever it takes place. For Italians, this is as often as possible, for *aperitivo* has become an integral piece of their national life and identity.

Aperitivo is less about what one drinks and more about how one does so.

Malloreddus with Sardinian lamb ragù

MALLOREDDUS AL RAGÙ DI AGNELLO

serves 4

On the island of Sardinia, locals often regale visitors with the quip *'Ci funti prusu brebeis de genti'* ('There are more sheep than people here'). This is not just a figure of speech: the island's three million sheep outnumber its human population of 1.6 million, which is unsurprising, for Sardinia is renowned throughout the gastronomic world for its pecorino Sardo, a cheese made from the milk of its special Sarda sheep.

Sardinia is a centre for slow-cooked lamb dishes, particularly in springtime, when the quality of lamb is exceptionally high and the meat at its most tender. The addition of fennel is common in some parts of Sardinia, where the herb grows freely. In this ragù, we prefer the heady trio of rosemary, mint and thyme.

1 tbsp extra virgin olive oil
600g lamb shoulder, cut into
*   1cm cubes*
1 small brown or white onion,
*   diced*
1 garlic clove, minced
1 large carrot, diced
1 celery stick, diced
500ml lamb stock
50ml red wine
800g quality tinned tomatoes,
*   chopped*
2 tsp caster sugar
1 tbsp chopped fresh mint leaves
1 sprig of fresh rosemary
1 bay leaf
2 sprigs of fresh thyme
500g malloreddus
Salt and black pepper, to taste
Parmesan, grated, to serve

1. Heat the oil in a large pan over a medium-high heat until it shimmers. Add the lamb and cook for 4 minutes on each side until nicely browned all over. Remove from the pan and set aside.

2. Add the onions to the fat that remains in the pan and cook over a medium heat for 4 minutes until soft. Stir in the garlic and cook briefly (no more than 1 minute) until fragrant.

3. Add the carrots and celery and cook for 5 minutes until softened. If the mixture starts to become dry, add a splash of lamb stock.

4. Add the red wine and let it bubble to deglaze the pan, scraping the brown bits from the bottom of the pan with a wooden spoon. When the wine has evaporated, add the remaining lamb stock and the tomatoes. Allow to simmer for 10 minutes.

5. Return the meat to the pan with the sugar, mint, rosemary, bay leaf and thyme. Simmer on a low heat for 1–2 hours, until the mixture has thickened and the lamb is very tender.

6. When the ragù has almost finished cooking, bring a pot of generously salted water to the boil. Cook the pasta until al dente, following the packet instructions.

7. Taste the sauce and season with salt and black pepper. Remove the sprigs of thyme and rosemary from the sauce and discard.

8. Once the pasta is al dente, drain the pasta and add to the sauce, stirring gently over a low heat for a minute or two before serving with freshly grated Parmesan to taste.

Pappardelle with Venetian duck ragù

PAPPARDELLE AL RAGÙ VENEZIANO

serves 6

When Italians speak of 'Veneto', they are not speaking of the city of Venice, but rather one of Italy's 20 regions to which the city of Venice belongs. The city of Venice itself is known in Italian as 'Venezia', and is merely one of Veneto's population centres. In this respect, it is important to recognise that Venetian cuisine refers to more than, say, the famous *cicchetti* ('small bites') enjoyed by locals around the canals of the relatively small city of Venice. Instead, Venetian cuisine is the sum of all of Veneto's towns, cities and villages. The pretty city of Vicenza, for example, is the birthplace of Veneto's quintessential *bigoli all'arna*. Bigoli are a long, thick pasta shape from the region, while *arna*, in the Venetian language, denotes duck. Curiously for a coastal region famous for its seafood, duck ragù is one of the defining – and undoubtedly most delicious – dishes of Veneto, and one we cannot abide missing out on whenever we visit.

2–3 tbsp unsalted butter
1 tbsp extra virgin olive oil
1 celery stick, finely chopped
1 brown or white onion,
  finely chopped
1 carrot, finely chopped
1 garlic clove, minced
500g duck breast, cut into 3cm
  cubes (save half of the duck's
  skin and dice this)
2 bay leaves
1 tsp cloves
1 cinnamon stick
100ml red wine
100–200ml vegetable stock
750g pappardelle
Salt and black pepper, to taste
Parmesan, grated, to serve

1. Heat the butter and oil in a frying pan and cook the celery, onion, carrot and minced garlic for 3–4 minutes until softened. Add the diced duck fat to the pan and render it for 4 minutes until it's browned.
2. Add the cubed duck breast, bay leaves, cloves and cinnamon stick to the pan, allowing the meat to brown for 4–5 minutes.
3. Deglaze the pan by pouring in the wine and allow the alcohol to evaporate completely (around 2 minutes). Add salt and pepper to taste and cook over a medium-low heat for about 30 minutes, adding the stock gradually whenever the sauce becomes too thick.
4. Bring a pot of generously salted water to the boil. Cook the pasta until al dente, following the packet instructions.
5. Once the pasta is al dente, drain and add to the ragù. Toss to combine, then plate and serve with some freshly grated Parmesan.

HOW TO MAKE FRESH PASTA DOUGH

EGG DOUGH

1. Place **500g of 00 flour** on a large wooden board.

2. Make a well in the centre of the mound of flour, large enough for **5 large eggs**.

3. Crack the eggs into the well.

4. Begin beating the eggs with a fork, slowly pulling in the flour from the sides of the well as you go.

5. As the mixture thickens, start using your hands to incorporate the remaining flour. You can also use a scraper to help loosen any extra bits of flour stuck to the board. Keep mixing with your hands until all the egg has been absorbed by the flour.

6. It's time to knead. Using the palm of your hand, knead the dough for 10–15 minutes until you reach an elastic consistency. If the dough feels too sticky, simply add a little more flour and continue to knead until it bounces back at your touch.

7. Leave to rest for 30 minutes, covered with a cloth or clingfilm.

VEGAN DOUGH

1. Place **500g of semola flour** on a large wooden board.

2. Make a well in the centre of the mound of flour, large enough to hold **200ml warm water**.

3. Start by adding half the water to the well, then begin to work the flour into the water with your fingers.

4. Add the rest of the water and continue to work the flour until all the water is fully absorbed.

5. Using both hands, push all the flour together and form a dough.

 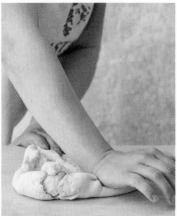 

6. It's time to knead. Using the palm of your hand, knead the dough for 10–15 minutes until you reach an elastic consistency. If the dough feels too sticky, simply add a little more flour and continue to knead until the dough bounces back at your touch.

7. Leave to rest for 10–15 minutes, covered with a cloth or clingfilm.

SEVEN SIMPLE SHAPES

ORECCHIETTE

1. Cut yourself a small piece of **vegan dough (see page 216)**; about one quarter is perfect. Leave the remaining dough to one side covered with a cloth or in a plastic bag.

2. Knead the small piece of dough for a few seconds to soften it.

3. Using the palm of your hand, carefully roll the small piece of dough into a long rope-like shape about 1cm thick.

4. Using a non-serrated knife, cut the rope into small pillows of dough around 1cm in length.

5. Take your first pillow of dough. With the round tip of a knife, press down on the top edge of the dough before dragging it along the work surface until it turns in on itself. Press your finger into the concave to make the shape into a dome.

6. Repeat with each pillow of dough.

7. Leave your orecchiette to dry on a clean tea towel or wire rack for a couple of hours.

MALLOREDDUS

 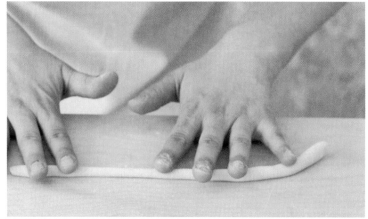

1. Cut yourself a small piece of **vegan dough (see page 216)**; about one quarter is perfect. Leave the remaining dough to one side covered with a cloth or in a plastic bag. Knead the small piece of dough for a few seconds to soften it.

2. Using the palm of your hand, carefully roll the small piece of dough into a long rope-like shape about 1cm thick.

 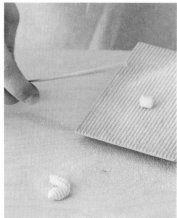

3. Using a non-serrated knife, cut the rope into little pieces, around 5mm in length.

4. Take your gnocchi board and place a piece of dough on top.

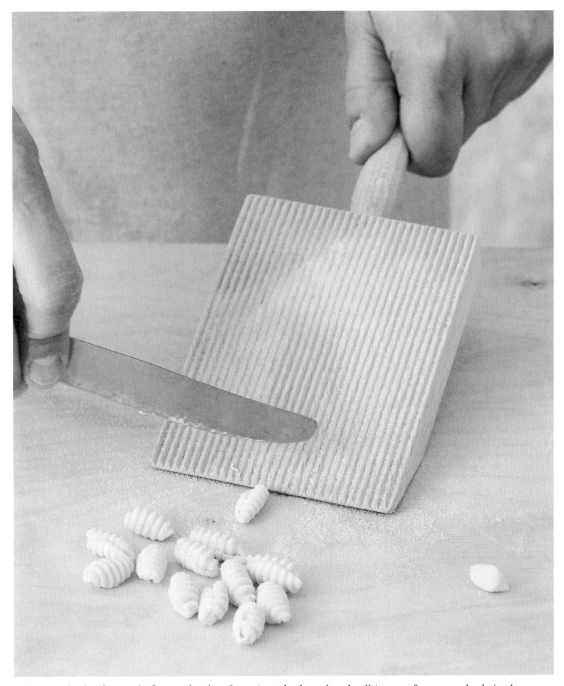

5. Using the knife, gently flatten the dough against the board and roll it away from your body in the direction of the grooves.
6. Repeat with each piece of dough.
7. Leave your malloreddus to dry on a clean tea towel or wire rack for a couple of hours.

TAGLIATELLE

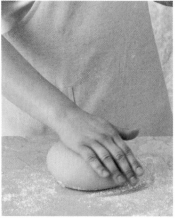  

1. Cut yourself a small piece of **egg dough (see page 214)**; about one quarter is perfect. Leave the remaining dough to one side covered with a cloth or in a plastic bag.

2. Place your dough on a wooden board and flatten it with the palm of your hand. You want it to be about 1cm thick (and no more than 2cm).

 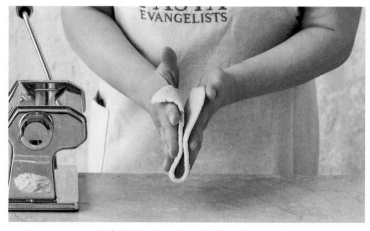

3. To prepare your pasta machine, place the rollers on the widest setting. This is usually setting 0 or 1, depending on the machine. Start to pass your dough slowly through the machine.

4. Once processed, fold the dough in half and repeat the previous step. Lightly flour the dough if it is sticking to the rollers.

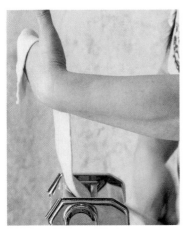

5. Reduce the space between the rollers by one notch. Continue to stretch the dough using your machine until it is approximately 3mm thick.

6. Adjust your pasta machine to the tagliatelle setting. Insert the dough and fold it through the machine until the tagliatelle forms.
7. Leave the tagliatelle to dry on a wooden board for an hour before cooking to attain a rustic texture.

SPAGHETTI

1. Cut yourself a small piece of **egg dough (see page 214)**; about one quarter is perfect. Leave the remaining dough to one side covered with a cloth or in a plastic bag.

2. Place your dough on a wooden board and flatten it with the palm of your hand. You want it to be about 1cm thick (and no more than 2cm).

3. To prepare your pasta machine, place the rollers on the widest setting. This is usually setting 0 or 1, depending on the machine. Start to pass your dough slowly through the machine.

4. Once processed, fold the dough in half and repeat the previous step. Lightly flour the dough if it is sticking to the rollers.

5. Reduce the space between the rollers by one notch. Continue to stretch the dough using your machine, until it is approximately 3mm thick.

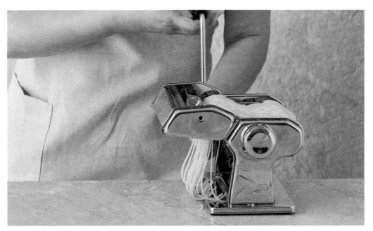

6. Adjust your pasta machine to the spaghetti setting. Insert the dough and fold it through the machine until the spaghetti forms.

7. Leave the spaghetti to dry on a wooden board before cooking.

PAPPARDELLE

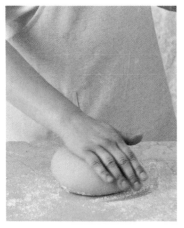

1. Cut yourself a small piece of **egg dough (see page 214)**; about one quarter is perfect. Leave the remaining dough to one side covered with a cloth or in a plastic bag.

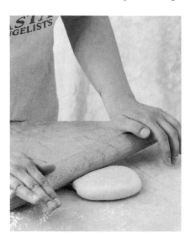

2. Flour the work surface. Using a rolling pin, start to roll your dough until it is elastic.

3. Keep rolling the dough until it is so transparent that you can see your hand through it. It should be about 2mm thick.

4. Sprinkle the dough with flour. This will prevent the pappardelle sticking together when cut.

5. Start to roll the dough inward from both sides, making sure you add extra flour as you fold so the dough does not stick together.

6. Once you have finished rolling the dough, cut the pappardelle into strips about 6mm wide.

7. Leave the pappardelle to dry on a wooden board for an hour before cooking to attain a rustic texture.

GNOCCHI

1. Place **300g of oo flour** on a large wooden board.

2. Make a well in the centre of the mound and add **1kg mashed potato** to the well.

3. Using your fingers, pull the potato into the flour from the centre. Crack **3 eggs** into the well.

4. Mix all the ingredients together using your hands. Once the egg is absorbed, you can begin kneading the dough for 10–15 minutes. After kneading the ball of dough, shape into a fat sausage (around 5–6cm thick).

5. Cut yourself a small piece of dough; about one quarter is perfect. Carefully roll the small piece of dough into a long rope-like shape about 0.75cm thick. Repeat this process for the rest of the dough.

6. With a non-serrated knife, cut the ropes into little pieces, around 5mm in length.

7. Take your gnocchi board and place a piece of dough on top. Using your finger, roll the gnocchi down the gnocchi board away from your body in the direction of the grooves. When you are finished, allow the gnocchi to rest on a wooden board for up to 1 hour before cooking.

RIGATONI

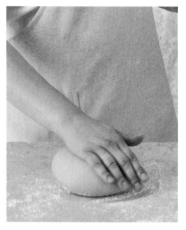

1. Cut yourself a small piece of **egg dough (see page 214)**; about one quarter is perfect. Leave the remaining dough to one side covered with a cloth or in a plastic bag.

2. Flour the work surface. Using a rolling pin, start to roll your dough until it is about 3mm thick.

3. Sprinkle the dough with flour. This will prevent the rigatoni sticking together when cut.

4. Cut the dough into long rectangular sheets, roughly 3cm wide.

5. From the long rectangular sheets, cut out smaller rectangles, each roughly 6cm long. Flour each rectangle well to avoid sticking.

6. Place a rectangle of dough on the board. Gently use the stick to roll it into a rigatoni shape, taking care with how much pressure you exert. It must be enough to create grooves but not enough to break the pasta.

7. After a couple of rolls, gently slide the stick out of the pasta.

RECOMMENDED SUPPLIERS

In Italy, most fresh ingredients are purchased at local markets where you have the opportunity to touch, smell and often taste them before buying. For this reason, we like to visit farmers' markets for fresh ingredients wherever possible. You can find your nearest market online.

If it's not possible for you to get to a market, or for ambient products, cheeses and pasta flour, we have included some alternative suppliers and stockists below. If you find it challenging to source a certain ingredient, you can also get in touch with us at chef@pastaevangelists.com and we'll do what we can to point you in the right direction.

ADIMARIA
[ADIMARIA.CO.UK]
Roberta buys her semola di grano duro here, used for making *pasta bianca* ('white pasta') such as malloreddus or orecchiette. You can also get your hands on gluten-free flour here.

DELICATEZZA
[DELICATEZZA.CO.UK]
Delicatezza is one of our favourite stockists. You'll find Italian cheeses such as stracciatella, burrata, fior di latte mozzarella and ricotta salata. As well as meats such as Calabrian 'nduja, fennel sausages, speck, prosciutto cotto and guanciale.

GASTRONOMICA
[GASTRONOMICA.CO.UK]
Gastronomica is another option for several Italian cheeses, including fontina, pecorino Romano, Taleggio and Gorgonzola.

NATOORA
[NATOORA.CO.UK]
Natoora is a shining beacon for fresh, seasonal vegetables and fruits in the UK. If you can't visit a farmers' market, Natoora has an array of produce through its app, but currently delivers only in London and other pockets within the M25. Fortunately, many of its products are also available on Ocado, with wider delivery.

SOUSCHEF
[SOUSCHEF.CO.UK]
Souschef offers lots of ambient ingredients of a high quality. You can find delicious tinned San Marzano tomatoes, for example, as well as our favourite brand of Mutti chopped tomatoes.

PASTA EVANGELISTS
[PASTAEVANGELISTS.COM]
Last but not least, many of the dishes in this book can also be bought directly from us as ready-to-prepare meal kits. We also carry a range of pasta-making kits, pasta chefs' aprons, and more.

INDEX

GRAZIE

To our co-founders Alessandro Savelli and Chris Rennoldson, for sharing in our limitless love of pasta and so patiently bearing with us as we wrote this book while carrying out our day jobs.

To our friend and colleague Sunita Patel, a source of endless wisdom, creativity and wit, and without whose input and support this book would not have been possible.

To Roberta's nonna, Maria-Assunta d'Elia, for teaching Roberta to cook as a little girl and instilling a life-long love of *cucina povera* and food. You are missed dearly every day.

To our editor, Ru Merritt, for championing our love of Italy, and pasta, from the day we met her. For her enthusiasm for this book and the stories and recipes in it.

To all those who contributed recipes, stories, snippets, or in any other way to this book: Imma Apuzzo, Martina Prinzis, Sophie Cobley, Belinda Davies, Siwan Lewis, Lia Mondavi, Jennifer Mitchell, and the rest of the Pasta Evangelists team.

To our photographer, Tim Atkins, for his indefatigable cheer, positivity and enthusiasm for Pasta Evangelists over the years. For his ability to capture pasta at its most beautiful.

To our food stylist, Emily Kydd, for being so characteristically patient with us as we continued experimenting with our recipes to the very last second, chopping and changing as we went. For her ability to make our food look so lovely, yet effortless and real, all at the same time.

To Finn's mum, Deanna, for patiently reading through countless drafts of this book (and for being one of the longest Pasta Evangelists subscribers).

To Roberta's partner, Francesco, for being a pillar of strength and reminding her that she could do it. For being Roberta's personal guinea pig for countless recipes over the years.

To Alessandro's mum, Ruth, for so generously proofreading the words written in this book.

To China & Co, for providing many of the beautiful plates, bowls and other bits and pieces used to bring the photographs to life. And for being so good about it when we broke a couple in the process!

To Stoke Newington Green Fruit & Vegetables, for providing much of the fresh produce used in the recipes featured throughout this book.

To Fin & Flounder, for providing much of the seafood used in the recipes featured throughout this book.

ABOUT THE AUTHORS

Pasta Evangelists is on a simple mission - to bring a taste of Italy's fresh pasta culture to British kitchens. Beginning as a subscription box in 2016, Pasta Evangelists has since delivered over 1 million boxes, with success coming from a focus on delivering fresh, homemade pasta, beautiful sauces and authentic recipes that will transport customers to Italy. Find out more at pastaevangelists.com

Roberta D'Elia is the Head Chef at Pasta Evangelists, born and raised in Puglia her favourite pasta shape is orecchiette. Finn Lagun is co-founder of Pasta Evangelists and his favourite pasta shape is paccheri.

CONVERSION TABLES

OVEN TEMPERATURE GUIDE

Elec °C	Elec °F	Elec °C (Fan)	Gas mark
200	400	180	6
220	425	200	7

LIQUID MEASUREMENTS (under 1 litre)

Metric	Imperial	Australian/US
25	1 fl oz	
60	2 fl oz	¼ cup
75	3 fl oz	
100	3½ fl oz	
120	4 fl oz	½ cup
150	5 fl oz	
180	6 fl oz	¾ cup
200	7 fl oz	
250	9 fl oz	1 cup
300	10½ fl oz	1¼ cups
400	14 fl oz	1¾ cups
600	1 pint	2½ cups
750	1¼ pints	3 cups
1 litre	1¾ pints	1 quart or 4 cups

WEIGHT MEASUREMENTS

Metric	Imperial
10	½ oz
20	¾ oz
25	1 oz
40	1½ oz
50	2 oz
60	2½ oz
75	3 oz
110	4 oz
125	4½ oz
150	5 oz
175	6 oz
200	7 oz
225	8 oz
250	9 oz
275	10 oz
350	12 oz
450	1 lb
700	1½ lb
900	2 lb

First published in Great Britain in 2021 by Seven Dials
an imprint of The Orion Publishing Group Ltd
Carmelite House, 50 Victoria Embankment
London EC4Y 0DZ

An Hachette UK Company

1 3 5 7 9 10 8 6 4 2

Text © Pasta Evangelists Limited 2021
Design and layout © Orion 2021

Images on pp.22-24, 62-63, 72-74, 114-115, 134-136, 178-179,
190-192 and 198-199 from Shutterstock

Editor: Ru Merritt
Photographer: Tim Atkins
Art Director and Design: Clare Sivell
Production Controller: Claire Keep

A CIP catalogue record for this book is
available from the British Library.

ISBN (Hardback) 978 1 8418 8475 2
ISBN (eBook) 978 1 8418 8476 9

Printed in Italy

MIX
Paper from
responsible sources
FSC® C023419
FSC
www.fsc.org

www.orionbooks.co.uk